STUDIES IN HISTORY, ECONOMICS AND PUBLIC LAW

EDITED BY

THE UNIVERSITY FACULTY OF POLITICAL SCIENCE

OF COLUMBIA COLLEGE.

Volume V]   [Number 1

DOUBLE TAXATION

IN THE

UNITED STATES

BY

FRANCIS WALKER, Ph.D.

Sometime University Fellow in Political Economy

THE LAWBOOK EXCHANGE, LTD.

Clark, New Jersey

2004

ISBN 1-58477-364-2

The quality of this reprint is equivalent to the quality of the original work.

Printed in the United States of America on acid-free paper

THE LAWBOOK EXCHANGE, LTD.
33 Terminal Avenue
Clark, New Jersey 07066-1321

*Please see our website for a selection of our other publications
and fine facsimile reprints of classic works of legal history:*
www.lawbookexchange.com

Library of Congress Cataloging-in-Publication Data

Walker, Francis, 1870-1950.
    Double taxation in the United States / by Francis Walker.
      p. cm.
    Originally published : New York : Columbia College, 1895. (Studies in history,
economics, and public law ; v. 5, no. 1)
    Includes bibliographical references and index.
    ISBN 1-58477-364-2 (cloth : alk. paper)
      1. Double taxation—United States. I. Title. II. Studies in history, economics, and public
law ; v. 5, no. 1.

KF6306.W35 2003
341.4'844'0973—dc21   2003052753

STUDIES IN HISTORY, ECONOMICS AND PUBLIC LAW

EDITED BY

THE UNIVERSITY FACULTY OF POLITICAL SCIENCE

OF COLUMBIA COLLEGE.

Volume V]   [Number 1

DOUBLE TAXATION

IN THE

UNITED STATES

BY

FRANCIS WALKER, Ph.D.

Sometime University Fellow in Political Economy

COLUMBIA COLLEGE

NEW YORK

1895

PREFACE.

THE present publication is the general part of a larger work which has been in preparation since the autumn of 1892. It includes a discussion of the problems of double taxation, particularly as they appear under the methods of direct taxation practiced in the United States. Reference is made to the actual facts to illustrate the discussion and to present a general view of the law and practice. Citations have generally been restricted in this place to some of the important cases, but in the detailed examination of the laws of each state, both statutes and decisions will be cited with extensive quotations. It is hoped to secure thus the greatest possible accuracy in the statement of the law. This detailed statement, revised to date, is now nearly completed.

No pretense is made to any great originality of thought, but it is believed that the classification is, in some repects, new, and that the discussion has been given a systematic form. In regard to the individual points of theory the writer has found that almost everything has been stated either positively or negatively in the multitudinous legal arguments and opinions.

This question has been treated in this country by Prof. Seligman, in his articles on " The General Property Tax " and " The Taxation of Corporations" in the fifth volume of the Political Science Quarterly. Numerous pamphleteers, especially in Boston, have discussed some of the questions fragmentarily. The reports of occasional tax commissions of the several states also give valuable material. In foreign countries little seems to have been done except in Germany and Switzerland, where federal complications similar to those in the United States are found. The principal works are by Zürcher, " Verbot der Doppelbesteuerung," and Schanz, " Die Steuerpflicht," in the Finanz Archiv, 1892.

In conclusion the writer wishes to express his obligation especially to Prof. Seligman, of Columbia College, under whose instruction he acquired his chief interest in financial questions, and at whose suggestion this study was undertaken. To Dr. Munroe Smith, Professor of Comparative Jurisprudence, and to Prof. Goodnow, Professor of Administrative Law, the writer also is deeply indebted.

BOSTON, *May 10th, 1895.*

TABLE OF CONTENTS.

PAGE

CHAPTER I.

Introduction, the importance of financial questions. Problem defined. Basis and nature of taxation, income or property, personal or material. Forms of double taxation within a state. Property and debts, property and income, property in its direct and representative forms (capital stock and "franchise," *etc.*). Double taxation arising from a conflict of jurisdiction. Considered in relation to politics ; the nature of political allegiance and jurisdiction. In relation to jurisprudence, the legal *situs* of property ; realty, chattels and *choses in action*. In relation to economics ; the actual productive force of the state and not consumption is the basis of taxation. Tabular analysis of personal liability to taxation. Question of incidence . .   9

CHAPTER II.

The federal form of the United States government and conflicts of jurisdiction arising thereunder. The taxing powers of the general government and the state governments and their constitutional limitations, expressed and implied. The growth and character of the tax systems of the general government and the state governments   36

CHAPTER III.

Property and debts ; the negative character of credit property. General and unsecured indebtedness. Book debts. Banking debts ; deposits. Mortgage debts. Corporation bonds. Public stock. Corporation shares ; *quasi* debts.   44

(vii)

PAGE

CHAPTER IV.

Property and income. General income taxes. Income
from particular forms of business; gross receipts and premium taxes. Income from privileged callings and occupations. Income from special kinds of property   69

CHAPTER V.

Property taxed twice. Capital stock taxes. Specific or
" excise" taxes on " franchise," *etc.* Specific taxes on privileged callings or occupations   79

CHAPTER VI.

Jurisdiction in taxation; property and persons. Considered, first, within the state; realty, tangible personalty and
choses in action. Considered, second, without the state;
the same. . . . ., ...   89

CHAPTER VII.

Jurisdiction in taxation; business and corporations. Considered, first, within the state; property taxes, capital
stock taxes, specific taxes and occupation taxes. Considered, second, without the state; the same   113

CHAPTER VIII.

Conclusion. The solution of the problem in accordance
with actual worth and economic *situs* depends on the
question of debt deduction and the taxation of the non-resident creditor. Debt deduction considered as to residents
and non-residents in respect to unsecured debts, mortgage
debts, corporate debts and public debts. Interstate character of the security of corporate debts and the exemption
of public debts make a satisfactory solution impossible.
Taxation of tangible property only, gives a consistent but
unequal result. Possibility of federal interference considered in regard to the taxation of non-resident bondholders.
Public securities should not be exempted from taxation. .   127

DOUBLE TAXATION.

CHAPTER I.

THE increasing complexity of modern social conditions and the actual magnitude of the interests involved have led to a demand for a more detailed consideration of financial problems. To this necessity we find no exception in the problems of taxation, which are perhaps the most difficult, as well as the most important, in the range of public law. Though these questions of taxation are, indeed, the only ones which have attracted any considerable attention from English and American writers, the treatment of them until recent years has been only of a very general character.

The present theme is an inquiry into the actual condition of the law in this country in regard to the question of double taxation. In taxation, next in importance to adequacy, in the view of public policy, is justice, and it often rises superior; for while inadequacy of revenue may embarrass and hamper a government, injustice in assessment will demoralize and corrupt it. ⁂ The most prevalent notion of justice in taxation is the requirement of equality; but, both in the ideas of justice and in the determination of equality, there are extremely divergent views. Double taxation is one form of unequal taxation. It consists either in taxing the same source of wealth twice in a given state, or in two different states taxing the same source of wealth.[1] The problems presented are two-fold

---

[1] *Cf.* Seligman, *General Property Tax*, Political Science Quarterly, v, 32; *The Taxation of Corporations*, Political Science Quarterly, v, 637.

and distinct—equality of law and conflict of law. Though in
one sense distinct, a solution of the problems should be found
by a consideration of their inter-relations.

It has been observed that the complex character of modern
society makes the necessity of a scientific determination of
financial problems especially important. In the subject of
double taxation it is particularly necessary, and its cause is
two-fold, corresponding to its two-fold character. On one
side, we observe that with the rapid advancement in material
civilization, especially in this country, an entirely new condition of things has been steadily evolved. The social constitution has become extremely intricate, the divisions of labor
have been multiplied, and great masses of people are segre-
gated in cities. The organization of industry under capital-
istic direction in great enterprises with stock companies, corporations and trusts, has completely changed the economic
conditions of the people. The three conspicuous facts are:
first, the enormous development of the machinery of credit
and its application to business, with the establishment of great
money-lending classes; second, the development of the corporation, necessitated by the vast scale on which modern
undertakings are conducted; third, the increase of the wage
and salaried classes, which is partly the result of the change
from agricultural conditions to those of trade, manufacture
and city life. On the other hand, with this increasing internal
complexity of the state, we find an equally great increase in
the intermingling of the citizens and residents of different
states, and a habit and practice of investment in all parts of
the world. The simple crudities of former times, of comparative unimportance, and unnoticed by the legislators,
become, by force of the interests involved, matters of great
social injustice. Enterprise no longer finds its limit within
state or even national lines, and possessions, especially of
great railway corporations, become inter-state and international.

For any solution of the present problem, a sound and practical philosophy of taxation is desirable; at least some definite standards for analysis must be established.

Taxation is a compulsory contribution exacted by the government for public purposes from persons or property. In this definition all kinds of taxes are included, but in the discussion of the question of double taxation, we are limited to the field of direct taxation. These contributions are levied on persons or property; that is, taxes may be *personal* or *real*. Considering the personal element first as the primary factor, what is the basis of contribution? Generally ability has been declared to be the proper test; and income, not property, the correct measure of ability. It is very clear that the taxation of property does not reach all the persons capable of paying taxes.[1] It may be asserted, also, that neither is income a perfect test. Some property does not yield income.[2] The income tax is, however, the one direct tax which has been declared by almost all economists to be the most just. Viewed from the personal standpoint, all persons owe the state a share of their income. The property tax exempts those vast numbers of persons who live on their income and accumulate no property. Its injustice is obvious. The sum total of the individual incomes should equal the total income. For, according to the income theory, the income of the state is the limit of taxation; so, also, it should be, logically, the basis.[3]

---

[1] Ely, *Report of the Maryland Tax Commission*, 1888, p. 177.

[2] This may be due to its nature or to the uses to which it is put. Examples of the former are the luxurious furniture of houses, costly jewels, pleasure grounds; examples of the latter are found in real estate held for speculation, investments of capital not yet arrived at the point of yielding returns, and investments which in unprosperous years fail to earn a profit. If ability of the individual is the test, the proprietors of such great and valuable properties are truly taxable, though this is sometimes denied. Such estates should be taxed on a basis of their actual present value.

[3] Is there any duplication under this system? On one side the taxation of personal service incomes would seem to cause it. On the other side non-productive property, which has value but yields no income, ought to be taxed.

We have seen what is the proper basis of taxation from a personal standpoint: let us now consider the question from a material or property standpoint. The first thing to be observed is that a tax is a material contribution. This implies private property. If there were no private ownership, the state would take from the property in its jurisdiction what it desired, irrespective of persons or places. Recognizing, however, private ownership, it is obliged to follow some rule in appropriating wealth to its use. It is plain that the practical limit to taxation is the net income of a community. This income may be viewed as a material net product, of which a part is saved, a part consumed. As net product or income, all is equally taxable. No accumulation of property is necessary; the government may take its share as it comes. So, also, if accumulated or saved and applied to future production, it is an economic source of income, and, as such, is on the same simple principle subject to taxation.[1] The state recognizes private ownership in applying some uniform rule to the taxation of the incomes derived from such property. In other words, the state taxes persons in proportion to their incomes.

So far in our examination the basis of taxation has been discussed on one side only, *i. e.*, the nature of the liability and its measure. Coördinate with this is the question, as to what persons or estates are taxable. Taking the personal view of the tax, it would seem that all persons receiving income who are found within the jurisdiction of the state would be subject. Taking, however, a purely material view, it would seem that all income derived from the property within the state would be taxable, and this, regardless of the fact of the non-residence of the person to whom such income accrued. The general tendency of jurisprudence is to substitute the territorial for the personal relation. Should this principle likewise control in taxation? More specifically, the question is whether the

---

[1] *Cf.* Bastable, *Public Finance*, p. 298.

property of residents shall be taxed if situated abroad, and the property of non-residents if situated at home.

Having reached certain conclusions with regard to the general subject-matter of taxation, and the jurisdiction thereof, we may now consider more particularly the subject of double taxation itself. As this discussion is preliminary to an exposition of the actual state of the law in the United States, a classification based on the forms of taxation most commonly prevailing has been adopted, that is, on the basis of a property tax. Considering the various specific cases arising independently in a single jurisdiction, we find that they may be grouped under three heads : first, property and debts ; second, property and income; third, property taxed twice.

A striking characteristic of modern society is the large amount of indebtedness owing by one part to another. Many of our legislators have declared that this is an additional source of wealth. It was a once popular theory, illustrated by the celebrated Jay Cooke in his " National Debt a National Blessing." That the tax-paying capacity of society is dependent on its realized wealth, and not its debts, is a truism. The best illustration of this fallacy is to suppose that in a given state all debts are suddenly paid, with the result of an immediate and equal reduction of the taxable valuation. It has been wittily said that to tax property and debts is " to tax, *not only ability, but liability*."[1] To say that debts do not increase the taxable property is one thing ; but it is quite another to say that therefore the *creditor* is not taxable on the debt due him. The correct theory seems plain. Tax each according to his worth : the liability of the debtor is the ability of the creditor. Let the debtor deduct from his taxable property that which he owes. To tax the full value of the property and also the debt, is clearly double taxation.[2] Yet this has not always been freely

---

[1] G. C. Crocker, *Double Taxation*, p. 6.

[2] Seligman, *General Property Tax*, p. 33.

admitted. The Maryland Tax Commission of 1888 thought that the argument was "not a good one."[1] The creditor, in fact, is, to a great degree, economically speaking, a co-partner in the possessions of the debtor. That debt is a claim on a certain portion of the debtor's property; it may be, on the one hand, only an imperfect or a general claim, or it may be, on the other hand, a matured or a particular claim. The security of the creditor may be indefinite, protected by the law and conditions of commercial credit in a general way, or it may be a definite claim, with a specific lien. The creditor is, therefore, not merely the owner of a piece of paper; he is to a greater or less extent the owner of tangible wealth, not in a legal but in a philosophical sense. Therefore, in taxing the debtor on the full value of the property, we are taxing him on something not wholly his.

The debts existing in a community may be viewed from an economic standpoint as, first, non-industrial; second, industrial; and third, *quasi* debts. By the non-industrial debts are meant, debts that are either not contracted with a view to economic gain (*i. e.*, non-productive), or that have lost that character (*i. e.*, where the basis of the debt has disappeared through waste, *etc.*). Here is found no economic justification for the debt, but if it is still solvent, it ought to be treated according to the general principle, with a deduction from the debtor's property. The industrial debt is a clear form and illustration of the inequity of double taxation. The debt is actually, and may be explicitly, recognized as a form of co-ownership of debtor and creditor. The creditor is a partner of limited liability and limited profits. The *quasi* debts are a form that arise from the existence of corporations. In this aspect, the essence of a corporation is that it is itself a person, artificial in character, which has distinct and separable relations with its component parts, composed of natural persons. The corporation is a debtor to its members.

[1] *Maryland Tax Commission*, 1888, p. 77.

The taxation of both property and income is a most obvious form of double taxation; but while in the case of the taxation of property and debts there is always from the nature of things double taxation, whether the taxation of property and income will be liable to such an indictment will depend on the nature of the system.   Income itself is always properly taxable, but when it is derived from property it cannot be regarded as a tax subject independent of that property.   The value of property, in general, is imputed from income therefrom obtained.   So it is evidently unjust to tax the whole once and a part twice, as would be the case with a general income tax and a general property tax.[1]   The possessors of property would pay two rates over a part of their income, *i. e.*, over that derived from property.   This seems indisputably to be a case of double taxation, yet the opposite view has been held apparently by most distinguished authority.[2]   You cannot classify individuals justly as property holders and non-property holders, because, income being the basis, there is but one class.[3] If property and income taxes both are used, the income tax should be general, with a deduction for property taxed, if double taxation would be avoided.   To tax "all income regardless of source, even if that source has already been taxed," may be a practical measure, but it is *primâ facie* unjust.[4]   Income taxes are special as well as general.   A special income tax may be laid on the revenues of property or the gains of business.   Disregarding questions of incidence, such taxes are unjust where they are not balanced by equal taxes on other sources of wealth or income.   Income taxes may be distinguished by their scope, and their modes of assessment and rating.   Practically, the chief forms are general income taxes, taxes on the gross or net receipts of business, and graded rates based on various criteria of income.

[1] F. A. Walker, *Political Economy*, p. 502.

[2] Seligman, *Taxation of Corporations*, Pol. Sci. Quart. v, 638.

[3] *Cf.* Bastable, *Public Finance*, p. 303.   [4] *Rept. Md. Tax Com.*, 1888, p. 183.

It has been seen that a general property tax and an income tax would not involve double taxation, if all income came from property. So, under a system of property taxation, two property taxes would not involve double taxation if they were levied on the same basis or in such a manner as to cover the same ground. This would be repetition, merely, without inequality. Specific double taxation of property, *eo nomine*, is seldom found, but there are two conspicuous kinds of taxation which shield themselves under economic fallacies or legal fictions. Such are some of the taxes on franchise and capital stock. Franchises consist of certain forms of actual property of an intangible nature, which are legal rights or privileges. Like debts, they are intangible, but they are distinguished from them by the fact that while debts have real value and virtue as property only through the existence of certain actual or tangible values on which the debt is a claim, franchises and similar properties have an existence independent of other property.[1] Illustrations of franchises are charter rights of corporations, patent rights, privileged occupations, *etc.*[2]

[1] In economics property is thought of as a thing, and may be divided as follows : Tangible property, *e. g.*, lands, cattle; intangible property, *e. g.*, notes, shares, franchises, *etc.* The legal view is more philosophical; property consists in a right or a congeries of rights which have an economic value. Thus, property in land is the right to exercise a certain control over it and reap its fruits; in a franchise, to do certain advantageous things; in a bond, to claim something valuable from another. Property is thus tangible and intangible, positive and negative. Debts have been termed negative, and are clearly so. But in a broad sense there is a negative in all private property Thus, in land, the use is restricted. Looking at a franchise, here also a social loss appears; perhaps it is a direct and conscious surrender of the free and " natural" activities of the rest of the community. The best example is the patent right. It is quite apparent again in certain rights, such as servitudes. The use of the term negative, as applied to choses in action, consists in this, that in so far as they involve a claim for tangible values from a private person, they are a deduction from his taxable ability; they are always a proper subject of taxation themselves, even when held against the public treasury, just as a franchise ought to be.

[2] Seligman, *Taxation of Corp., op. cit.*, 438, *et seq.*

Franchises of real value are, of course, properly taxable.[1] This has been admitted by the advocates of the doctrine of taxation of tangible things.[2] The state would be guilty of injustice in exempting them. They are often treated, however, in quite a different manner. By calling a tax a franchise tax, an arbitrary valuation may be made and grossly double taxation produced. Engaging in certain occupations may be declared to be a privilege, without any just economic ground for the distinction, and thus the person pursuing it be doubly taxed. An important point in the franchise tax is the determination of the valuation. There are many methods adopted, and generally they are arbitrary, or at least purely empirical. The true franchise value is something superadded to the property. Where the franchise is held by a corporation, the total value of franchise and property is generally ascertainable with considerable accuracy. Subtracting from the total value the value of the tangible property, gives us an amount which may be said fairly to represent the value of the franchise. So, similarly, we can often apply this principle to individuals. The sale of the good-will of a mercantile house or of a professional practice is a familiar example of the valuation of intangible things of this character.

The taxation of capital stock is another common form of double taxation. To tax the property of a corporation and also its capital stock, broadly speaking, is taxing the property twice. The property and capital stock of a corporation are not, indeed, always identical,[3] and in many corporations far from it; but the capital stock always stands in some measure for the property.[4] To tax the capital stock, where the property is also taxed, and to declare it to be legally another kind of property, or to call the tax a franchise tax, does not justify it.[5] The

---

[1] *Md. Tax Com. Report*, 1888, pp. 17–18.

[2] Wm. Endicott, *The Taxation only of Tangible Things.*

[3] Seligman, *Taxation of Corp., op. cit.*, p, 447.

[4] *Ibid.*, pp. 642–3.   [5] *Ibid.*, p. 449.

actual relation of capital stock to the tangible property varies. The real taxable value of a corporation is the tangible property plus the franchise. Where no liability exists, the value of the capital stock will correspond closely with it. But if liabilities exist, they diminish the value of the capital stock, proportionably. If we should add the debts to the capital stock, the actual value of the property would be approximately determined.[1] We may express this idea in an equation: Capital stock + debts = tangible property + franchise. In certain cases the equations will stand: Capital stock = tangible property + franchise, or : debts = tangible property + franchise. The first is perhaps the normal condition of manufacturing corporations ; the second is often the predicament of certain other corporations,[2] especially railroads.[3] It is a notorious fact that many railways are built on their bonds, and that their stock represents the value of the franchise only, which is of course largely speculative at first. Applying this analysis to the problem of taxation, it is plain that a capital stock tax and a tax on the tangible property may, or may not, according to the circumstances of the case, involve taxing a greater actual value than exists. If the debts equaled the tangible property the equation might read: Capital stock = franchise. In that case, the taxation of both the capital stock and the tangible property would not only not involve double taxation, but would represent the actual value of the total property. Conceivably, also, it might represent less. But, in general, it may be safely assumed that to tax both capital stock and tangible property is double taxation in a large degree.

The second part of our subject deals with the taxation of the same property by two different jurisdictions. The question

---

[1] Seligman, *Taxation of Corp.*, *op. cit.*,p. 452; *Md. Tax Com. Rept.*, 1888, p. 19.

[2] Pacific Hotel Co. *vs.* Lieb (1876), 83 Ill., 602.

[3] *Md. Tax Com. Rept.*, 1888, pp. 18, 19.

may be viewed in its three principal aspects—political, legal and economic. We have to deal here with the nature of political allegiance, the conflict of law and the economic relations of persons to the communities in which they live or hold property.

What is the nature of political allegiance, and does this affect the principles of taxation? The state is based on two concrete objectivities, territory and people.[1] The first is by its nature fixed, the second is in flux. The control of the state over its territory is complete and absolute, but over the individuals of its population it is conditional. A state may lose control over the latter through emigration. As a practical ground for citizenship, birth has given place to residence; governments have become territorial instead of personal. The state can fix upon any principle consistent with its character for the basis of taxation. Its will is supreme, and the duty of the citizen is correspondingly great. The limitations of the taxing power are two: depending, first, upon the physical circumstances of the state; second, upon its purpose. The state cannot take more than it actually possesses, nor that beyond its actual jurisdiction or control; this is a natural·limitation.[2] It is further limited by its purpose, which is justice.

When the citizen or subject of a state removes to another state, he withdraws his person from its control, and if he also transfers his possessions, he exempts them likewise. To reach his person, it is necessary that the subject return.[3] A similar rule prevails as to persons coming into the state.[4] The property must also be within the territory of a state to be subject thereto, and an actual *situs* therein is sufficient to establish jurisdiction.[5] The law in recognizing this has merely accepted

[1] *Cf.* Burgess, *Political Science*, p. 50.

[2] *Cf.* Opinion of Justice Agnew in Washington Ave. Case, 69 Pa. St., 352.

[3] Story, *Conflict of Laws*, § 540.

[4] *Ibid.*, § 541.   [5] *Ibid.*, § 539.

positive facts. There would be no difficulty were it not that the person may live in one state and hold his property in another. The opportunity is thereby created for the state which has jurisdiction over the person to exercise compulsion in order to obtain the property. Of course such attempts may conceivably fail, demonstrating the real lack of power. But, apart from the question of power, the end of the state is justice, and there can be little doubt that as to those forms of property which are incontestably without the state, the most enlightened opinion is opposed to taxing them. This has been said to be "the only upright course."[1] "The practice of taxing property outside of the territory and jurisdiction of a state merely because the owner is a citizen or resident of the state, rests upon identically the same principle as that which constitutes the basis of brigandage, namely that the control of the person of the victim confers the right to a revenue consisting of a percentage of the value of all the victim's property of every description and wherever situated."[2] Good authority doubtless exists for the other view; but this much is evident, that no solution of the problem of double taxation will ever be made on such a basis.[3] If the avoidance of double taxation be of sufficient importance to determine the question, then the country of actual *situs* should, without doubt, be awarded the power of taxation.[4] The taxation of property abroad, held by a resident, may be justified, however, on grounds of expediency, or speaking more precisely, of financial advantage. Thus has the policy of Massachusetts been upheld.[5] Under what theory is this justified?

There are two chief theories respecting the basis of taxation

---

[1] Seligman, *Taxation of Corp., op. cit.*, 650.

[2] *Report of the New York Tax Commission*, 1872, p. 22.

[3] *Cf.* Bastable, *Public Finance*, p. 304.

[4] *Cf.* Seligman, *Taxation of Corp., op. cit.*, pp. 647–8.

[5] *Mass. Tax Report*, 1875, pp. 106–7.

—the "personal obligation" theory and the "protection" theory.
The protection theory is the classic one of political economy,
but of late years it has become more and more discredited.[1]   It
still occupies a prominent place, however, in our judicial decisions.   It was a great exaggeration, therefore, the assertion
of Mr. Wells, that "taxation implies protection.   It is held
by every authority to be the equivalent for the protection
which the government affords to the property of its citizens."[2]
The "protection" theory made the payment of taxes a payment
for value received, in the protection of the person or the property of the taxpayer.   But no civilized system of taxation ever
regulated the rate of its assessments on this basis.   The protection theory may claim to have more plausibility in another
way, *i. e.*, the fixing of the proper place of taxation.   The protection of property shows the virtual relation of the state
thereto.   But the difficulty is that this is also applied to persons.   "The old protection theory would say that the country
of residence should be paid for guarding the person, and that
where the property lies for watching over it."[3]   The defect of
the doctrine, as applied, consisted in the fact that it was often
used to maintain the liability of the resident for all the property he possessed at home or abroad, and to justify the taxation
of the non-resident on his property lying in its borders.   The
"personal" theory demands that taxation should be rated
according to the ability of the tax-payer, because it is his duty
to pay what he can, equally with his fellow-citizens; of course,
this payment is due to the state of which he is a member.   This
is an elevated idea, and it is certainly a relatively true basis
for the rating of taxes, as long as the citizen's property is
within the state.   But, if a part of the sources of his income be
from property abroad, then a modification must be made in

---

[1] Cossa, *Taxation*, p. 54.

[2] *N. Y. Tax Commission Report*, 1872.

[3] Bastable, *Public Finance*, p. 304.

the theory, or the tax-payer will be subjected to double taxation, because even the extreme personal view would never be carried so far as to demand the exemption from taxation of non-resident lands. The Massachusetts Tax Commission of 1875 held that the basis of taxation was social necessity,[1] and that it should be levied according to ability, extending this even to extra-territorial property.[2]

The personal theory has been upheld by most modern writers. It is said that " we must disabuse ourselves of the idea that property, as such, owes any duty to pay taxes. The State has direct relations not with property but with persons."[1] Of course, it is evidently true that property, as inanimate matter, has no moral duty ; but the state certainly has relations with property in many ways, and in taxation as well as others. Those who claim the necessity of a personal view in regard to taxes would often be among the first to demand some adjustment between conflicting jurisdictions, and would not be disposed to agree to the exemption of the tangible property of non-residents within the state. When the state exacts a tax from the land, it deems it immaterial who the owner is. The non-resident landowner is not taxed, because he has personal or political relations with the community ; he pays the tax because it is assessed on the land.[4]

The subject of jurisdiction, when considered from a legal point of view, is full of difficulties. Taxation, however, as a practical problem, depends so much upon the attitude of the law and the necessary legal limitations, that a general and brief

---

[1] *Mass. Tax Report*, 1875, p. 10.   [2] *Ibid.*, p. 105.

[3] Seligman, *The General Property Tax, op. cit.*, p. 56. "An die Spitze stellen wir den Satz, dass die Steuerpflicht stets eine persönliche ist; sie wendet sich immer an Personen ; gegenüber einem Objekt oder einer Sache kann keine Pflicht geltend gemacht werden."—Schanz, *Finanz-Archiv.*, 1892, ii, s. 3.

[4] In the recent legal developments, this view in regard to land taxes is illus trated by the abandonment of the formal method of assessment to owners, whether known or unknown, and the substitution of the method of taxation *in rem*.

consideration of the same is necessary. The general statement is that the force of the law of a state is absolute within the confines of its territory, as to persons resident therein or to property situated in it; on the other hand, it is of no validity as against persons resident without its borders or to property lying in another state.[1] "(1) Every state is entitled to demand that its own laws only shall be recognized within its bounds. (2) No state can require the recognition of its laws beyond its bounds. I will not only admit the truth of these propositions, but even allow their extension to the utmost conceivable limits."[2]   The assertion of jurisdiction over all persons within the territory, by any state, necessarily involves a denial of the jurisdiction ot any other state. The rule applies in a broad sense to every person, of no matter what nationality or citizenship, who may sojourn there, though international law recognizes the actual interest that a foreign state may take in its citizens abroad, and for mutual convenience may allow modifications of the rule; but this depends upon convention or comity. Apart from this, however, no authority of a foreign state is recognized.[3] Personal statutes may be enforced against a citizen after he returns to his country, but not while abroad. The degree to which the jurisdiction over the person may be exercised, to control his property abroad, is disputed. Of course it can be enforced only through the person, by duress, *etc.*; and the decrees of a court, in that case, would have no standing in the courts of any other country, least of all in the country where the property was actually situated.[4]

As to property, "the laws of the place where such property is situated, exclusively govern in respect to the rights of the parties."[5] This may be stated as universal; the divergence lies

---

[1] Story, *Conflict of Laws*, § 539.

[2] Savigny, *Conflict of Laws*, Guthrie's translation, Edinburgh, p. 26.

[3] Story, *Conflict of Laws*, §§ 540, 541.

[4] *Ibid.*, § 543.   [5] *Ibid.*, § 424.

however in the interpretation of the law of *situs*. There are, in this respect, two kinds of property distinguished—immovable and movable. As to the former, jurisdiction follows *situs* invariably; "every attempt of any foreign tribunal to found a jurisdiction over it must, from the very nature of the case, be utterly nugatory, and its decree must be forever incapable of execution *in rem.*"[1] The term immovable is subject to legal interpretation. The law recognizes not only land and the physical fixtures attached thereto, but also real rights following the land such as "servitudes and easements, and other charges on lands, as mortgages and rents, and trust estates."[2] This is merely the extent of the general doctrine of jurisprudence. The local law may modify it so that "all other things, though movable in their nature, which by the local law are deemed immovables, are in like manner governed by the local law. In other words, in order to ascertain what is immovable or real property, we must resort to the *lex loci rei sitae.*"[3] Of course the local law may, contrariwise, declare things naturally immovable to be movable.[4] It is in the theory of movables that we find the greatest divergence. Movables themselves are properly subdivided into tangible and intangible personalty; for many purposes it will be found that the law as respects tangible personalty is much nearer that controlling realty than to intangible personalty. This is on account of the practical difference of actual and constructive *situs*. For certain general purposes of the private law of property, *e. g.*, transfer, alienation, disposition, *etc.*, the prevailing doctrine is that personalty has its *situs* at the residence of the owner; in other words, personal property has for these purposes no independent locality.[5] There are some limitations on this: first, in the nature of

---

[1] Story, *Conflict of Laws*, § 551.

[2] *Ibid.*, § 447.   [3] *Ibid.*, § 447.

[4] *Cf., e. g.*, Ill. R. S., 1891, ch. 120, §§ 14, 15, gas mains, street railways, bridges.

[5] Story, *Conflict of Laws*, § 376.

the property itself, such as give it necessarily a local character; and secondly, those of " positive or customary law of the country where they are situate."[1] Proceedings *in rem* against personal property may be had only in the country of actual *situs*, and the disposition of those courts is everywhere recognized.[2] In any case, no contract concerning such property contrary to the prohibitions of the *lex situs* will be valid anywhere.[3]

Turning now to intangible personalty and obligations, we find the accepted doctrine is that they have " no *situs* or locality; and they follow the person of the owner in point of right (*mobilia inhaerent ossibus domini*) although the remedy on them must be according to the law of the place where they are sought to be enforced."[4] In regard to this doctrine, the following is an often quoted passage of the same distinguished authority: " Although movables are for many purposes to be deemed to have no *situs*, except that of the domicile of the owner, yet this being but a legal fiction, it yields whenever it is necessary for the purpose of justice that the actual *situs* of the thing should be examined. A nation within whose territory any personal property is actually situate has an entire dominion over it while therein, in point of sovereignty and jurisdiction, as it has over immovable property situate there. It may regulate its transfer, and subject it to process and execution, and provide for and control the uses and disposition of it, to the same extent that it may exert its authority over immovable property. One of the grounds upon which, as we have seen, jurisdiction is assumed over non-residents, is through the instrumentality of their personal property, as well as their real property, within the local sovereignty. Hence it is that whenever personal property is taken by arrest, attachment or execution within a state, the title so acquired under the laws of the state is held valid in every other state, and the same

---

[1] Story, *Conflict of Laws*, § 383.

[2] *Ibid.*, § 592.   [3] *Ibid.*, § 373.   [4] *Ibid.*, § 362.

rule is applied to debts due to non-residents, which are subjected to the like process under the local laws of the state." [1]
The doctrine in regard to personal property has constantly
tended to lay more and more emphasis on the actual *situs*. In
a note to Story's Conflict of Laws, the editor says : "The
exceptions to the maxim *mobilia sequuntur personam* have become so numerous that it cannot be safely invoked for the decision of any but the simplest cases at the present day ; if
indeed a case can ever be safely decided upon a maxim. The
exceptions would probably be less frequent if the maxim were
lex situs mobilia regit. . . . Of course for the purpose of taxation the *lex situs* will prevail."

Apart from the actual power of a state to regulate such matters for all kinds of property, if it undertakes to do so, certain
particular forms of obligations have (as has been already stated
of personal property generally) in a special degree an independent *situs*. That is, in the legal view there is a marked distinction between credits of various sorts. Story cites Lord Mansfield as holding that this may be affirmed of " contracts respecting the public funds or stocks, the local nature of which requires
them to be carried into execution according to the local law,"
and he continues: " The same rule may properly apply to
all other local stock or funds, although of a personal nature,
or so made by the local law, such as bank stock, insurance
stock, turnpike, canal and bridge shares, and other incorporeal
property owing its existence to or regulated by peculiar local
laws. No positive transfer can be made of such property except in the manner prescribed by the local regulations." [2] The
question of negotiability is important. Choses in action, such
as shares of stock, that have only a restricted negotiability
may be given an independent *situs*, but this would be impossible where mere endorsement or manual delivery passed the
ownership. [3] Other forms of property which might be sus-

[1] Story, *Conflict of Laws*, § 550.   [2] *Ibid.*, § 383.
[3] *Cf.* Tax Collector *vs.* Insur. Co., (1890) 42 La. An., 1172.

ceptible to similar treatment under appropriate conditions are corporation bonds, bank deposits and mortgages.

The third consideration, in respect to taxable jurisdiction of property, is the economic one. The economic principles are the foundation, in a large measure, of politics and law, but the positive institutions of the latter also react to modify and even to control in many details the economic conditions. No system of taxation can be founded and long endure on a fundamentally unreal economic basis; yet if in the main part real, an immense amount, positively considered, of divergence therefrom may be tolerated, though, to a corresponding degree, it forms an element of weakness in the state. Philosophically, the taxation strength of a state is dependent on its powers of production. This is applicable to any conception of the state or community, whether we consider its external relations or its inner constitution. An "isolated state" finds its taxing power measured by its annual income; a communistic state looks to the same source for its expenditures.[1] There are in the conditions of modern international life, certain facts which plainly modify this view.

But, before proceeding to consider them, it is desirable to notice that one other great basis for taxation exists, which is, however, not wholly independent of the primary one, *i. e.*, consumption. Consumption, is not a rational basis of taxation in any large sense. It represents neither the capacity of the state nor the ability of the individual with any high degree of truthfulness. But it is, nevertheless, an important practical form; it may also be, in view of the imperfections of administration of the laws, and of certain other complications,

---

[1] "Die Steuergewalt findet ihr Genüge innerhalb des eigenen Territoriums; die Güter, die aus diesem hervorgehen, sind zum principalen Steuerfond gestempelt; das ist der Bereich, wo die Zwangs- und Kontrollmittel am wirksamsten sind, das ist der Bereich, über welches auch sonst der Gemeinschaftswille in der Regel nicht hinausgreift, innerhalb dessen er sich aber möglichst voll und ganz geltend macht."—Schanz, *Finanz-Archiv*, 1892, ii, s. 9.

a useful and relatively just one. The complications which afford a reason for the partial use of consumption taxes are those arising from the international confusion of productive agencies, and the local concentration of creditor classes, the same which, in some degree, make expedient a modification of the productive basis of taxation.

Let us make a more particular analysis of this subject. First, as to the productive capacity; what does that include? Reconsidering the discussion of the questions of double taxation as they arise in a particular state, it is maintained that the total positive wealth, tangible and intangible, or the total income, is the proper basis; that debts are in no sense an addition to this, but merely represent an interest of the creditor in such wealth; that the creditor is properly taxable thereon, as on any other property value. It will also be remembered that from the view of political justice, it was held that the non-resident holding property therein was rightly taxable. The logical consequence of this is that a non-resident creditor of one state is not taxable on such credits in the state of residence. That it may be impracticable, or even impossible, to tax the non-resident creditor is no refutation of the theoretical value of the argument. That an approximation to justice, a partial avoidance of double taxation is desirable, any improvement, in fact, on the present system, will not be disputed. But, as a matter of fact, there is a vast amount of this indebtedness which can be taxed to the non-resident creditor, beside which the part which would escape would be, under a proper system, of minor importance. The great examples are stocks, bonds and mortgages.

Another matter, not yet specially considered, demands attention here. Income has been used as a term more or less convertible with property, and it has been insisted that such incomes as are not derived from property are taxable. But the question of their *situs* has not been discussed. From its nature, income from services is associated with or attached to the person ; there is no separation in an economic sense. The same is undoubtedly true in both the political and legal view. When, however, such a person shall perform his services in different places, he is liable at each one on the same grounds. Agents are subject to the same rule as principals. This brings us to the proper point to consider certain incomes which may be dependent on property values in one place, yet might be said to be derived also, to a certain extent, at a central administrative place in another jurisdiction than the property. For example, a corporation whose wealth is directly invested in material wealth producing property, as a railroad, may have its property in one state and its principal office of administration in a great commercial center in another jurisdiction, on account of the business advantages derived therein. New York City is the headquarters of many corporations doing business in other states. Of course the service incomes of its officers, who are engaged there, including perhaps its directors, president, *etc.*, are there taxable, and this would not in any way affect the general propositions advanced. The question is whether a foreign railroad, for example, is doing business there in a degree sufficient to make it taxable. Perhaps a slight tax on franchise is justified, and in that case a deduction, theoretically, should be made from the taxation of franchise value, where the road is situated; but this is, evidently, very vague and quite unsatisfactory.

The exemption from taxation, on their property situated in other states, of wealthy residents of a city, may appear to be, to some extent, an unfair limitation on the state of residence, and in a still greater degree as respects the municipality of residence.[1] The resident, it may be presumed, finds there greater benefits and enjoyments and, it may be claimed, should pay for them as well as the rest of the community. The claim

[1] In the tax systems of the several states, however, this method is often quite completely carried out as respects the property of its citizens within its borders.

undoubtedly derives particularly great force where expenditures for general convenience, health and pleasure are very extensive. It is true that a part of this is met by such persons in the taxes they pay on the real and personal property held and used there and also in their contributions through special assessments. On the other hand there are large net advantages to the community in the attraction of such persons, who promote the material prosperity of the city in many ways. It may be held, however, that these persons are not adequately taxed. One method of remedying this defect has been proposed by Dr. Schanz who suggests that the place where the property lies or the income accrues should tax three-fourths of the value thereof, and the place where the person resides should tax one-fourth.[1] Apart from the arbitrary character of this division, it seems objectionable as depriving the community of productive acquisition of a portion of its proper tax material.

Consumption taxes of various kinds might be levied in order that persons residing within the state, but owning no property, nor deriving any income therein, might contribute their share. Inheritance taxes might also be used for that purpose. A more practicable expedient might be found in the expansion of the system of special assessments.

Relying then on the principles stated above, a classification may be made, and the taxability systematically tabulated. We shall first make a general division based on the source of production, whether within or without the state, at home or abroad; under this we shall next consider residence or non-

---

[1] " Wenn und insoweit Wohnsitz (bezw. Konsumption) und Einkommensquelle auseinanderfallen, ist die wirtschaftliche Zugehörigkeit geteilt; zum kleineren Teil fällt sie der Konsumptionsgemeinschaft zu, zum grösseren und intensiverer Weise derjenigen Gemeinschaft, in der die Einkommensquelle liegt, wo der Erwerb sich vollzieht. Desshalb dürfte hier eine passende Norm sein, wenn das Gemeinwesen der Einkommensquelle ¾ und das Gemeinwessen des Wohnsitzes ¼ der nach seinen Bestimmungen schuldigen Steuer in Anspruch nimmt."— Schanz, *Finanz-Archiv.*, 1892, ii, s. 11.

residence as the next most important circumstance; finally, and of least significance, whether the person be a citizen or alien.

Tabulating on the above basis we have:

I. Property (or income therefrom) situated in the state.
　　1st, held by a resident who may be,
　　　　(*a*) a citizen, or
　　　　(*b*) an alien.
　　2d, or held by a non-resident, who may be,
　　　　(*c*) a citizen, or
　　　　(*d*) an alien.
II. Property (or income therefrom) situated without the state.
　　3d, held by a resident, who may be,
　　　　(*e*) a citizen, or
　　　　(*f*) an alien.
　　4th, or held by a non-resident, who may be,
　　　　(*g*) a citizen, or
　　　　(*h*) an alien.

There can be no doubt that the property in a state of a resident citizen is taxable (*a*): there is certainly no other taxable jurisdiction.　Property in the state of a resident alien (*b*): this, to a large extent, is taxed by all states, and needs no justification.　Property in the state of a non-resident citizen (*c*): whether the tax system is based on nationality or territory, liability is clearly established here, at least for all tangible property.　Property in the state held by a non-resident alien (*d*): this is also taxable; political citizenship cannot be held to be superior to the fundamental economic conditions of society.　Hence we again conclude that all property in a state is taxable, by whomsoever possessed.　The property held abroad by a resident citizen (*e*): this is often considered taxable.　It is the reverse of the case of property held within the state by a non-resident alien; that was held taxable, and if double taxation is to be avoided. this should be deemed exempt.　The state should choose one rule as to taxation and not two contrary ones, to gain a financial advantage. If indeed such property were not taxable at its actual *situs*, some degree of justice might be asserted. Perhaps this would apply, for example, to property in barbarous lands. Even in semi-civilized countries, where extra-territorial jurisdiction is largely exercised, there may be some practical justification. Property abroad of a resident alien (f): that the alien is taxable may be readily admitted, but not on property held without the state. The jurisdiction of the state over him is based on a material fact; its right to tax him has the same limits. Property without the state, held by a non-resident citizen (g): to consider this taxable the most rigorous basis of citizenship would be required, which no nation could consistently adopt. Property held abroad by a non-resident alien (h): the state has no right whatever to tax such property and it has not generally the power; rationally it is not open to discussion. Hence we find again that in every case property without the state is not justly taxable.

Property situated within the state, or the revenue derived therefrom, or business done within its confines, should form the basis of taxation. Regarding the state itself, we recognize that this constitutes its actual economic strength. That the property is owned by a non-resident, or the income received from property or business goes to a person residing without the state, should not be allowed to diminish the state's power of taxation, even though it may be felt that it is necessary to thus permit the diminution of its wealth. The alien who invests his wealth in property within a state, of his own free will, joins in the economic life of the community; he acquires property and revenues therein under the laws of that community; his rights to obtain it, to keep it, to transfer it, are all by its authority and consent. It may refuse to let him enter its borders, it may banish him thence, and it may deprive him of that property which he has acquired situated within its jurisdiction. In levying a tax, the state merely appropriates

that portion of its property which it finds necessary for its purposes. It cannot recognize that the ownership of an alien,
which it has permitted, forms any bar to its expropriation if it
sees fit. And though the state may for its advantage do so,
yet this would be foreign to the most elementary principles
which lie at the basis of just and scientific taxation. It would
be proper only in exceptional circumstances. The object
sought in levying the tax is to absorb from its territories and
possessions such revenue as it deems necessary. It is immaterial to the state, in a certain sense, whether the funds are
obtained from public domain or from private owners. The tax
is above all other considerations material. The basis of the
tax is by logical necessity a material basis; in its broadest
terms, it is the aggregate of the economic productivities within
its jurisdiction. To adopt therefore a basis of citizenship, of
caste or class, or of residence, is utterly inconsistent therewith.

Before proceeding to the particular consideration of the
subject in the United States, it is necessary to note certain
necessary limitations to the discussion of the problem, which
are both theoretical and practical. Tax systems must be first
of all efficient for the purpose of producing revenue, and the
minor details of equality are often necessarily subordinated.
Therefore, it cannot be expected that a uniform or even perfectly consistent method will be adopted. Superior, also, to
absolute equality are questions of public policy, by which a
confessed discrimination is often made in order to gain or pre-
serve more important advantages. But, apart from this practical view, to which we shall return again later on, there are
questions of economic theory which make this problem
very much more abstruse from a purely theoretical standpoint.
It is evident that any discussion of double taxation is concerned only with direct taxes, by which is meant taxes such
as are levied on property, incomes or occupations, with the
expectation that the burden will lie on the person assessed.
Consumption taxes, therefore, though they may be used, are

not open to discussion, simply because it would be impossible to arrive at any definite conclusions. They might be investigated experimentally, perhaps; but, beyond the conclusion that they were almost invariably unequal in burden, no result would be arrived at.

With direct taxes it is otherwise, yet, even here we are met by complicated problems of incidence. In general, for the purposes of this inquiry, it will be assumed that the taxes are borne by those who pay them, that when the law has levied an equal and universal tax on the abilities of persons, such a tax is, in fact, an equal burden, unless there are particular reasons for further discussion. No treatment of taxation is adequate which does not keep in mind this difficult question, yet it may be granted that a solution of the *primâ facie* forms of double taxation is first desirable. It is the very vagueness of the general opinion on this subject, and the appeals to unscientific doctrines of incidence, that are largely responsible for much unequal taxation that exists at present. The doctrine which has seized the popular mind with greatest force is that taxes diffuse themselves. This forms a convenient defense for any system of taxation. This doctrine was broadly asserted by the New York tax commission[1] in their report in 1871 and again in the report of 1872. It was stated in the latter as an absolute and invariable principle. The Commissioners say " they further maintain that *all taxes equate and diffuse themselves, and that if levied with certainty and uniformity upon tangible property and fixed signs of property, they will, by a diffusion and repercussion, reach and burden all visible, and also all invisible and intangible property, with unerring certainty and equality*."[2] Usually, however, such extreme doctrines have received little recognition. In the United States, this fact is conclusively shown by the attempts to tax all property. But it has been commonly advanced to support particular propositions, as, for example, that

[1] *Report*, 1871, p. 26. [2] *Ibid.*, 1872, p. 47.

a tax on mortgages is a tax on the borrower, and that in no manner can it be virtually collected from the lender. This was maintained by the Maryland Tax Commission of 1880.[1] The Massachusetts Commission took a more scientific position in declaring that " in certain cases taxes will undoubtedly equalize and diffuse themselves; but as a uniform doctrine it is condemned by facts, and justified by no sound economic theory. Instead of diffusing themselves, the tendency of taxes is to stay where they are laid; in other words, the tendency is that they must be paid by the actual persons upon whom they are levied. . . . Moreover, if the diffusion of taxes be granted in a given instance . . . the important question arises whether this diffusion is an equal and a just one . . . it can hardly be doubted that in this shifting process a disproportionate burden always falls upon the poor."[2] Perhaps the next most noteworthy idea is that taxes are capitalized in the property taxed, so that a permanent discount continues on the selling value, by which fact the subsequent purchasers are virtually exempt. This doctrine is historically associated with the English land tax liquidations. Recently an important application of the principle has been made to the theory of the taxation of corporate indebtedness.[3] A discussion of the merits of these questions, as well as of the problems of incidence in general, beyond this passing notice, would be inappropriate here, and it has been most ably treated elsewhere.[4]

[1] *Report*, 1888, p. 75.
[2] *Mass. Tax Com.*, 1872, pp. 22-4.
[3] Seligman, *Taxation of Corp.*, *op. cit.*, 674.
[4] *Cf.* Seligman, *On the Incidence and Shifting of Taxation.*

CHAPTER II.

In the United States the problems of double taxation are evidently of peculiar importance. The fact that each of the forty-four States of the Union has independent powers of taxation results in a conflict of law to which no other nation, except the German Empire and the Swiss Confederation, can afford a parallel. The federal government has its conflicts with other nations; it has also its relations with the various commonwealths that divide its territory; and these again have their conflicts, not only with the nations of the world, but also with each other. There are other taxing authorities within the United States; but their authority is delegated, and not original. The taxes levied by the territorial governments are authorized by acts of Congress. The taxes levied by the counties, municipalities, and other subordinate political organizations of the commonwealths, are authorized by the laws of their respective legislatures. In the systems of taxation practiced by these delegate bodies, naturally there can be no conflict of jurisdiction; there may be, however, internally unequal or double taxation arising from the application of improper principles. That double taxation may exist under the system practiced by the federal government, as respects the determination of taxable subjects within its jurisdiction, is evident, and these come properly within the scope of this inquiry. It is also clear that double taxation may exist as between that system and those practiced by other national governments, and here a complete discussion would necessitate an examination in detail of their systems. As to the relation of the federal system to those of the commonwealths, it is not a matter of conflict; that the citizens are taxed by both authorities

involves no double taxation, since the jurisdictions are properly concurrent.[1] The systems, both national and state, may
be, however, themselves unequal internally. Apart from
the fact that both jurisdictions are independent, the circumstances are the same as in cases of inconsistent taxation of
commonwealths and their municipalities. As to the commonwealth systems of taxation, it is clear there is a conflict of law
as between them and foreign nations, and also, in a similar way,
between each other. Their relation to the national government has already been referred to. Within their own organization minor delegate taxing bodies exist, such as counties,
cities, towns, villages, school districts, *etc.* In the commonwealth system, and also in these delegated systems, may exist
forms of taxation which are contrary to the canons of equality.
But the matter is then strictly internal.

The taxing power of the United States, within the constitution, is sovereign and unlimited; so, also, the taxing power in
the commonwealths is plenary, except as limited by their own
constitutions and the constitution of the United States. The
constitutional limitations are absolute, and bind both the federal
government and the commonwealths. The limitations of the
federal constitution are of two kinds; first, those expressed in
the letter of the constitution; second, those implied from the
purpose of that instrument. In the first class are the provisions
that Congress shall not tax exports;[2] shall not levy any direct
or capitation taxes, except by apportionment, according to the
population in the several states;[3] and that all taxes shall be
uniform throughout the United States;[4] and as respects the
states only, that they shall not levy any tax on exports or imports, or levy tonnage duties without the consent of Congress.[5]

In the second class, *i. e.*, the limitations implied in the instrument, the first general restriction is that neither the federal gov-

---

[1] *Federalist*, no. xxxvi.   [2] *U. S. Const.*, art. I, § 9.

[3] *Ibid.*, art. I, § 9.   [4] *Ibid.*, art. I, § 8.   [5] *Ibid.*, art. I, § 10.

ernment nor the commonwealth shall embarrass the other in the exercise of its constitutional powers.[1] This is a necessary implication. It has been said by high authority that "the power to tax involves the power to destroy; that the power to destroy may defeat and render useless the power to create; that there is a plain repugnancy in conferring on one government a power to control the constitutional measures of another."[2]

Whatever may be thought of the absolute correctness of the first proposition, it can be confidently asserted to be good political science and good political economy, as well as settled law, that neither the federal government nor the commonwealths should tax the public property of the other. It is also justly maintained that they should not tax the public processes of law and administration, or any property or privilege or action which has a purely public end and distinct from private gain; further, that any institution or agency established for public advantage, but which, at the same time, is an instrument of private gain, should not be taxed in respect to that private interest, in a manner which shall discriminate against it, and thus embarrass the proper measures of the government establishing it. This, however, is the proper limit of this doctrine, certainly, from an economic standpoint, and the political argument in support of this limitation becomes every day of increased weight.[3] The courts have not stopped here, but have extended it in a manner not logically demanded by the principle, inconsistent in itself, and at the same time in violation of the dictates of science, and of the just rights of the other governments. The discussion of this topic cannot be further pursued here, except to note its bearing on the present subject. For so far as these exemptions are established, equal distribution of taxation on the incomes of the persons or property taxable is made impossible.

[1] Cooley, *Law of Taxation*, p. 83.

[2] Marshall, C. J., in McCulloch *vs.* Md. (1823), 4 Wheat., 316.

[3] *Cf.* Thompson *vs.* Pacific Ry. Co. (1869), 9 Wall., 579.

The conspicuous examples of complete or partial exemption which fall under this limitation are the property of either government, the bonds,[1] notes and debts of the United States,[2] which are by law exempt, the property of the national banks,[3] the franchises[4] granted to corporations, the salary of United States and state officers, and the property in patents granted by the United States ;[5] of these the exemption of some is admittedly proper, of others, decidedly not.

In regard to commerce there are positive restrictions which have been already noted. The prohibition of the commonwealths from taxing imports and exports has been extended in interpretation to include certain other taxes which are not such directly. This is the case, for example, with taxes on auctioneers' sales of imported goods,[6] which are forbidden on the ground that " a tax on the sale of an article, imported only for sale, is a tax on the article itself," and " a tax on the occupation of an importer is, in like manner, a tax on importation." The court has set the limit, as to the period for which imported goods retain their quality as imports, to the time they remain in unbroken packages.[7] The application of this legal principle to the constitutional prohibition is not satisfactory. It compels the exemption of certain classes from occupation taxes. Where, however, the purpose is police regulation, as the license of vendors of imported liquors, the right of the state has been affirmed.[8]

[1] Weston *vs.* Charleston (1829), 2 Peters, 449 ; Bank Tax Case (1864), 2 Wall., 200.

[2] Bank *vs.* Mayor, 7 Wall., 16 ; Bank *vs.* Supervisors, 7 Wall., 26.

[3] *Rev. Stat. U. S.*, § 5219.

[4] California *vs.* Pacific Ry. Co. (1887), 127 U. S., 1 ; Dartmouth College *vs.* Woodward (1819), 4 Wheat., 518, Opinion of Story, J. ; State R. R. Tax Cases (1875), 92 U. S., 575.

[5] Webber *vs.* Virginia (1880), 103 U. S., 344.

[6] Brown *vs.* Md., 12 Wheat., 419.   [7] *Ibia.*

[8] License Cases (1847), 5 How., 504 ; *cf.* Cooley, *Taxation*, p. 12.

Congress is given power to " regulate commerce with foreign nations, and among the several States." The states retain their original right to regulate their internal commerce,
and at first it was thought that they had also the right to regulate inter-state commerce, within their own jurisdiction, in so
far as such regulation was not repugnant to the regulations of
Congress.[1] Taxation may of course be considered a method
of regulation, and as such, under the above supposition, capable of being exercised both by the federal and state governments. But it has been decided that the non-exercise of the
power to regulate, which the Constitution gives to Congress, is
merely a declaration that it shall be free.[2] This is good political science, if not good constitutional law. The importance
of the topic here lies in the application of the principle. A
tax on freight has been held to be a tax on commerce, being
in the nature of a duty on the articles transported.[3] A tax on
gross receipts of a railway has, however, been held to be lawful, since the tax was in the nature of an excise tax on the
corporation, and was paid from property actually possessed by
the corporation.[4] But this latter decision has been impugned
by recent authority; a tax on gross receipts for freight carried
through the state, though collected wholly or partly elsewhere, and held outside of the state by a foreign corporation,
was declared to be a tax on inter-state commerce.[5] Similarly
of the receipts of a steamship company, the tax was held to be
virtually a tax on commerce. " Taxing is one of the forms of
regulation. It is one of the principal forms. Taxing the
transportation, either by its tonnage or its distance, or by the
number of trips performed, or in any other way, would certainly be a regulation of the commerce, a restriction upon it, a

[1] *Cf.* Gibbon *vs.* Ogden, 9 Wheat., 1.

[2] Welton *vs.* Mo. (1875), 91 U. S., 275; Cooley, *Taxation*, p. 94.

[3] Reading Ry. Co. *vs.* Penna. (1872), 15 Wall.. 232.

[4] Reading Ry. Co. *vs.* Penna. (1872), 15 Wall., 284.

[5] Fargo *vs.* Mich. (1886), 121 U. S., 230.

burden upon it." [1] In the taxation of the business of telegraph companies, it has been held unconstitutional to tax messages sent beyond the state, since that is " a regulation of foreign and inter-state commerce." [2] The messages must be between points within the state. [3] ·As to express companies, a tax on gross receipts within the state was upheld. [4] It may be readily seen that some of these distinctions, often of no economic value and quite foreign to the spirit of the constitution, may operate to make unequal even a just system of taxation.

The power of taxation in the commonwealths, except in, respect to those matters in which the Federal constitution intervenes, are the same as those of an independent state. Of course the government of the commonwealth may be limited by its own constitution. There is also historically another limitation, which cannot be found in the constitutional limitations, either state or federal, but which has been announced by the Supreme Court of the United States. The states are denied the right to tax the choses in action of non-residents secured by property within the state, on the ground that such property is not within the jurisdiction of the state. [5] The court undertook to dictate to the state of Pennsylvania what were the proper subjects of taxation. [6] There seems good ground and authority for believing that this was an usurpation of power; there can be little question that the decision .was a grave economic blunder. [7] Four justices dissented from this opinion, *viz.*, Justices Davis, Clifford, Miller and Hunt. Davis, J., in giving the dissenting opinion, said : " I am àlways of opinion

[1] Phila. & So. S. S. Co. *vs.* Penna. (1887), 122 U. S., 326.

[2] Tel. Co. *vs.* Texas (1881), 105 U. S., 460.

[3] West. U. Tel. Co. *vs.* Seay (1890), 132 U. S., 472.

[4] Pacific Ex. Co. *vs.* Seibert (1891), 44 Fed. R., 310.

[5] Foreign Held Bonds Case (1872), 15 Wall., 300.

[6] *Cf.* Cooley, *Taxation*, p. 5.

[7] *Cf.* Seligman, *Taxation of Corp.*, *op. cit.*, p. 653.

that a state legislature is not restrained by anything in the federal constitution, nor by any principle which this court can enforce against the state court, from taxing the property of persons which it can reach and lay its hands on, whether these persons reside within or without the state."

The commonwealths are bound not only by the provisions of the federal constitution, in the matter of taxation, but also, in a more important and particular manner, by the state constitutions. The general provisions of these instruments are that taxation shall be uniform, and that it shall be levied on all persons or property. This however is not true of all. Other provisions sometimes found are that taxation shall be *ad valorem,* that it shall be proportional, or that it shall be equal on all persons in the same class.

The taxation of the federal government has been generally indirect, *i. e.,* through duties or imports and internal revenue excises. Of these we need speak no further. But there have been direct taxes laid at different times. The first direct taxes on lands, houses and slaves, were levied three times, and apportioned in the manner provided by the constitution. There have been also excise or license taxes on certain occupations, which, however, were hardly direct taxes. The chief direct taxes which have been levied by the federal government are the income taxes. These were first established during the war, but shortly after abolished. Within the past year the income tax has been revived.

The systems of taxation in the several states have a more remote origin, and an extremely diverse history. Suffice it to say that whether the original system was principally composed of capitation, excise, property, or other taxes, the general tendency in all states was to adopt the taxation of property as the central feature. All the states at present have a general property tax. This is supplemented by other taxes, such as poll taxes, taxes on occupations or sales, license taxes, *etc.* The taxes on occupations often occupy a prominent place in the sytem, and sometimes are of almost equal importance to the property tax. This is the case in some southern states. Income taxes are rarely found, and only as subordinate features. This may be said to be the condition also of the different commonwealths in the first half of the century. But with the growth of great corporations, of railroads, banks, insurance companies, and others, a demand more or less general appeared for special forms of taxation. Beginning in New York and Pennsylvania, and gradually spreading into other states, the special taxation of corporations was developed.[1] The principle was not everywhere accepted, however; and though the existence of corporations generally necessitated peculiar modes of valuation and assessment, the property valuation, as such, was not discarded. In some cases the differences are traceable to peculiar constitutional provisions and their judicial interpretation.[2] Often special methods are adopted to obtain a just taxation of a corporation possessing great amounts of exempted property.[3] This is very commonly seen in the taxation of savings banks.[4] The inter-state complications, and the conflicts of taxing authority, in respect to corporate property, especially of railroads, telegraph companies, pipes lines, express companies, mining and manufacturing corporations, have led to specialization also. One other form of taxation, though not of recent origin, that has become general only within the last few years, is the inheritance or succession tax. This originated in Pennsylvania, and, like the corporation taxes, was for a long time unknown to most of the other States. It was also a part of the " war" tax system of the general government.

[1] *Cf.* Seligman, *Taxation of Corp.*, p. 270, *et seq.*, pp. 298-9, *etc.*, *op. cit.*

[2] *Cf.* Commonw. *vs.* Hamilton M'f'g. Co. (1866), 94 Mass., 298.

[3] Home Insur. Co. *vs.* State (1890), 134 U. S., 594.

[4] Provident Inst. *vs.* Mass. (1867), 6 Wall., 611; Soc. for Savings *vs.* Coite (1867), 6 Wall., 594.

CHAPTER III.

PROPERTY AND DEBTS.

THE taxation of property and the deduction of indebtedness has been a subject of great controversy in this country. The fact that taxation is on property, and not on income, made the question open to dispute. As to income taxes, at least in a civilization advanced beyond the feudal stage, where tithes prevail, there can hardly be any question that the basis of taxation is on *net* income. The reason for this is that all income taxes look in a more direct manner to the persons receiving the income than to the sources from which the income is derived. With property taxes, however, the idea is much more mixed. The tax on property may be easily regarded as a charge upon things and not upon persons. In fact, this is often the acknowledged principle. It is particularly obvious in land taxes.[1] Taxes on land have been said to be " a sort of first claim on its revenues regardless of ownership."[2] This idea is applicable to personal property also. In fact, the tax process in some states is held to be a process *in rem*, and the obligation a real obligation.[3] A remarkable example of the application of this principle in the taxation of choses in action may be here referred to. In Connecticut, the holder of a mortgage or other taxable security may pay a certain definite

[1] *Cf. N. Y. Laws*, 1885, ch. 411.

[2] Ely, *Maryland Tax Com.*, 1888, p. 183.

[3] *Cf. Va. Acts*, 1889–91, ch. 244, § 1; Wright *vs.* Merriwether (1874), 51 Ala., 183; Varner *vs.* Calhoun (1872), 48 Ala., 178; Dreake *vs.* Beasley (1875), 26 O. S., 315; Perry *vs.* Washburne (1862), 20 Cal., 318; People *vs.* Seymour (1860), 16 Cal., 332; Glasgow *vs.* Rowse (1869), 43 Mo., 479.

percentage of the value as the tax thereon, and the fact of such payment is then inscribed on the paper, and the security is exempt for such period as the taxes have been paid.[1] Now, if taxes are viewed as real charges, it is evident that the problem of debt deduction becomes at once extremely difficult. It is clear that the mere fact that the owner of land is in debt on his personal bond gives no direct basis for the reduction of the taxes assessable against such land. If, however, the debt is secured by tangible values, it is not merely a personal obligation, but also a charge upon the security, so that, for the purposes of taxation, it would not be wrong in principle to look upon the interest of the creditor as a sort of co-ownership. Of course, where the debt is not secured by tangible property, the theoretical as well as the moral claim of the debtor to receive a deduction is the same. Moreover, in actual practice, the creditor may look to the same property of his debtor for the assurance of his reimbursement, although he may not deem it necessary to demand its legal hypothecation.

It is evident that the theory of debt deduction is based on the principle that the creditor is the real property-owner to that extent. That is, credits are property. This is now so commonly taken as a matter of course that the statement might seem superfluous. But it has not always been viewed in that light. The property characteristics of credits are certainly various in their assimilation to the characteristics of the complete ownership of tangible property. If our conception of property is purely material, the difference is very marked. The owner of property owns a thing, the owner of a credit owns a claim to a thing of another, either a particular thing or a thing of a certain kind. If our idea of property is that it is merely the right to exercise certain powers in respect to things, then the distinction between certain credits and the ownership of property is not so great. Now in this country the ordinary view is undoubtedly the former, *i. e.*, the thing

---

[1] *Conn. Pub. Acts*, 22 June, 1889, § 9.

not the right, is thought of. In some extreme cases, the opinion has been that credits were not property at all. This matter was a subject of controversy in Ohio.[1] In California, the court, after a period of disagreement and uncertainty, decided that choses in action were not property; it was held to be contrary to the meaning of the constitution. The court said: " The legislature may declare that a cause of action shall be taxed, but a cause of action cannot pay the tax . . . it is only the actual wealth to which government can resort."[2] Under the new constitution they are expressly taxable. In regard to the charter rights of municipalities in Virginia and North Carolina, it has often been decided that the right to tax property did not include credits. Credits have been taxable, however, in Massachusetts for nearly 250 years.[3]

Deduction of debts and the taxation of credits are clearly demanded, if equality of taxation is aimed at; but the practical difficulties are great. In the first place, where the debt is unsecured, the deduction must be made from the general property of the debtor. In the second place, it may be positively or practically impossible to tax the creditor; that is, the creditor may reside in another jurisdiction, or if he is within the jurisdiction, he may be able to evade the search of the assessors. The rule is sometimes made, therefore, that debts owing non-resident creditors shall not be deducted ; but this maims the equality of the assessment. As to the difficulty in taxing those who try to evade their just burdens, no adequate remedy has ever been found which will apply to all forms of indebtedness, and particularly to purely personal obligations. In consequence of these evils, therefore, there is a widespread opinion that only tangible property should be taxed. It seems manifestly unjust, however, to allow large moneyed classes to

---

[1] *Cf.* Exchange Bank *vs.* Hines (1853), 3 O. S., 1.

[2] People *vs.* Hibernia Bk. (1876), 51 Cal., 543.

[3] *Mass. Records*, iii, 220 (1651).

go free from taxation, even though they can be taxed only imperfectly. Moreover, as a matter of practical difficulty, the constitutional requirements of most states, that all property shall be taxed, oppose to this demand very great though not insuperable barriers. Leaving some of the subjects here referred to for further discussion later, we may now proceed to the investigation of the particular forms of indebtedness and the laws relating thereto.

Concretely considered, debts have many forms, such as notes, bills, accounts, deposits, mortgages, public and private bonds, and shares in corporations. These may be conveniently classed for discussion under the following divisions, *viz.*, general and unsecured debts, book debts, mortgage debts, banking debts, public and corporate bonds, and corporate shares.

General and Unsecured Debts. Deduction of indebtedness is the general rule in the tax systems of the states, though in about twelve states no deduction at all is permitted, as, for example, in Pennsylvania, Georgia, Maryland, Louisiana, Kentucky and Missouri. The extent to which deductions are permitted varies greatly. In New Jersey debts may be deducted from all property, real and personal; in New York and Connecticut from personal property only; in many cases deduction is allowed from moneys and credits, and in a few States from moneys on hand, as, for example, in Minnesota, North Carolina and Nebraska. Deduction from property is not permitted in New Jersey, if the creditor is a non-resident, and in California and South Dakota the debts owing to non-residents are not deductible from credits. The chief idea of the legislators seems to be to relieve the debtors from their excessive burdens; *i. e.,* the debtor is relieved from a certain amount of taxation with only an indirect reference, as a rule, to the taxation of the creditor on the values so exempted. Deductions are generally limited to moneys and credits. Apart from questions of policy, this is inconsistent and illogical. Debts and credits in the aggregate must, of course, balance; but, when the individual is considered, even an approximate cancellation is extremely improbable. Persons most heavily indebted have frequently no credits whatever.

Considering the practical aspects of the question, it is not to be doubted that the property should be taxed, even if inequality results, rather than any deduction should be allowed which was not compensated for in the taxation of the creditor. When credits are of such a character that they can escape detection and assessment, obviously deduction should not be permitted. It might be thought that, in so far as the debtor reveals the debt and the creditor, the deduction should be allowed. Probably with proper legislation this could be accomplished with considerable success (as between residents of the same state). Certainly no debts should be deducted without such information, nor should the debtor be acquitted of all liability for the value of the deduction made, until the same had been collected of the creditor. It would be a help towards bringing the creditor to bear the burden justly belonging to him. Yet it is undoubtedly true, that the matter of debt deduction is not satisfactory as applied to unsecured and unregistered debts. The opponents of the property tax have attacked it from this point; " deduction for debts is thoroughly pernicious in its operation. . . . Debt exemption and no debt exemption are equally bad."[1] The assessors of New York stated that debt deduction is " the cause of far more inequality and oppression than it remedies, and that no great improvement in the system of our taxation is possible until it is abolished or essentially modified."[2] The claim generally made is that credits cannot be found, and, therefore, any law taxing them " from the very necessity of the case never can be effectually carried out and enforced."[3] This assertion, as will be

---

[1] Seligman, *Gen. Prop. Tax*, p. 34.

[2] *Rept. Assessors*, 1882, quoted in *Rept. of Counsel to revise the Tax Laws of N. Y.*, pp. 8, 9.

[3] Wells, *Report of the N. Y. Com.*, 1871, p. 34.

seen more clearly later, is of very different degrees of correctness as applied to the various forms of credits. Others demand
that there shall be no deduction for debts, and declare that " a
man should pay taxes upon the full value of all he owns,
whether or not he has borrowed money in order to acquire or
retain it. He posssssses, occupies, uses and exercises dominion
over it, and expects the same protection and consideration
from the state for it, as if he owed nothing upon it, and he
ought to make to the state the same return for it." [1]

Book Debts. The theory that the tangible and intangible
property of a person, less his debts, constitutes his true taxable worth, may seem to be clear, yet the difficulties in its
practical application are in some cases extremely great.
This appears perhaps most conspicuously in the case of merchants and manufacturers. The merchant's total wealth consists of his tangible real and personal property and his credits,
minus his liabilities. But it may be impracticable to get a true
return of these things. The proportion that each item bears
to his total wealth is constantly varying, and his total wealth
itself is subject to violent fluctuations, and also in many instances difficult to value with any great degree of accuracy.
A serious complication is found in the fact that so much
business is done on borrowed capital. It would be extremely
difficult to disentangle all these relations.

Another point should be noticed; there is a great difference
in the quickness of sales. In one business the stock of goods
is turned over twice and even more times a year. In another
business there is but one conversion. It appears, therefore,
that the stock of goods at the beginning of operations is not a
true criterion, nor at any other time; that the total annual
stock is not correct either, since the same capital may be
converted once, twice, or perhaps more often ; that the average
amount on hand is not a true test, not only because the original stock was not, but also because with the rapid conversions

[1] *Maryland Tax Com.*, 1888, p. 77.

the average would probably be very much higher. The true property basis would be ascertainable only by an omniscient tax assessor.

The Maryland Tax Commission of 1888 was opposed to any deduction of debt from property.[1] Logically following out this idea, they proposed that all stock in trade should be taxed. " The average stock carried by a merchant during the year shall be taken to represent his actual worth, on the ground that to tax book accounts also is double taxation. If a man chooses to buy on credit we believe he should be taxed upon the full value of what he has bought, but if he has both bought and sold on credit we do not think it is just to tax him upon all he owes to others and all that is due to him."[2]

The taxation of stock on hand has been sometimes opposed apart from the equities of taxation. It is asserted that this leads to the emigration of trade elsewhere. " So far as it is tangible, it is exempted in its chief form, as stock in trade, by every intelligent official."[3] But it should be remembered that, in the first place, such exemption is not always tacitly allowed, and that, secondly, the same argument may be applied with equal force to other methods of taxation, such as income taxes, or to the taxation of the capital stock of corporate trading companies.

Owing to the transitory character of the ownership of merchants and manufacturers in their stock in trade, and the peculiar importance of indebtedness in their businesses, special methods of assessment have been frequently provided. Generally they are taxable on their credit accounts and stock in trade, as in Massachusetts, Indiana, Kentucky, Wisconsin and Texas. It is frequently provided that where the stock is assessed the average amount shall be taken, as for example in Alabama, Connecticut, Iowa and Ohio; in Wisconsin it has

---

[1] *Md. Tax Com.*, 1888, p. 77.   [2] *Ibid.*, p. 16.

[3] Seligman, *Gen. Prop. Tax*, p. 27 ; *cf. Md. Tax Com.*, 1888, p. 14.

been declared unlawful to tax the average value of the stock.
The average value of the credit accounts is sometimes taken,
as in Kansas and Wisconsin. In Alabama, where the average
amount of stock is taxed, it is provided that this must not be
less than the capital employed in the business; in Louisiana
the average value of the capital, both cash and credit, is taken.
In Missouri credits accruing from the sale of stock are not
taxable for the year during which they were contracted. Deduction is allowed for debts in most of the states referred to
above, except in Georgia, Kentucky, Louisiana and Missouri.
The methods of taxation of merchants and manufacturers
according to their stock in trade and credits seem full of difficulties. Perhaps the most practical solution is to assess the
average value of the stock in trade and take no account of
credits or debts. This is obviously inconsistent with an accurate assessment according to ability; but it is not the only
case where the most practical justice can be attained only at
the expense of theory.

Banks and Bank Deposits. The taxation of banks and similar institutions forms a special feature of the tax systems of
many states, and indeed was one of the first parts to be differentiated. It is, therefore, convenient to treat these laws separately, even where they are not in principle of a peculiar
character. As the regulations concerning banks usually give
a fairly complete oversight of their transactions—their deposits, their credits and debts, and other matters—it may be
practicable to enforce a theoretically equitable assessment.
From the principle that each party should be taxed according
to actual ability, it follows that banks should be taxed on their
property, less their liabilities. The liabilities of a bank are
three-fold: first (if it be a bank of issue), its notes; second, its
bills payable; third, its deposits. Its assets are its property
and bills receivable. Since the notes are of a peculiarly invisible kind of property, it may be conceded, without great incon-
sistency, that there should be no attempt to tax them to the

holders, but, instead, let the property which the bank receives therefor bear the direct burden. The notes themselves, of course, must be redeemed either by that property or other property of the bank. In the case of ordinary bills payable, we have the general case of credits. They should be deducted from the property, or assets, under a theoretically perfect system. The deposits are the property of the depositors, economically, however the legal ownership may be viewed. They should be taxed to the economic owner. In any case, they should not be taxed to both, directly or indirectly. The most general form of taxation of banks of discount and deposit is on the shares of capital stock. As the shares of capital stock are valued according to real value of the net assets of the bank, it is evident that no deduction need be made from them. On the other hand, the creditors of a bank, that is the depositors are properly taxable. It is evident that such indebtedness is a matter of record, and can be easily ascertained and taxed to the creditors.

Practically all the states tax the incorporated banks located therein on their shares of stock. Private banks are usually taxed on their property. In that case it is customary to provide that deposits shall be deducted from the credits of the bank, as, for example, in Illinois, Indiana, Michigan, North Carolina and Texas. Sometimes the deduction is allowed from all the property, as in Iowa and Ohio. In such cases, the depositors are taxed on their deposits. Savings banks in New Jersey and Massachusetts are taxable on their deposits, and the depositors are not liable. In New York, on the other hand, savings banks are not taxable on their deposits, but the depositors are liable. In Connecticut, except for certain exemptions, both are taxable. In some states unincorporated banks are taxed on their capital, as, for example, in Georgia, Kansas, Missouri and Wisconsin. Whether double taxation will arise depends upon the method of valuation practiced by the assessors. In Kansas it has been held that deposits are to

be included, and the court said that there was no more reason
why they should be deducted in assessing the property of the
bank than deductions should be given to merchants in assessing their stock on account of their indebtedness.[1] Generally,
however, it seems to be understood and admitted that the taxation of deposits to the bank and to the depositors is double
taxation.[2]

Mortgages. The general theory that taxation of both
property and debts is double taxation, applies as clearly to
mortgages as any class of property. As a matter of fact, it is
one of the chief forms of double taxation that is widely recognized, and sometimes has been treated as though it were *sui
generis*. Though theoretically no different from other debts,
it is, nevertheless, of greater practical importance because,
first, it is connected with the taxation of land ; second, its value
is secured by a definite lien, even though the obligation may
be at the same time personally binding ; third, it is practicable
to require the registration of mortgages; fourth, the law of
situs controls the nature and form of the instrument, its
validity and its enforcement.[3] Positive law, moreover, can
declare mortgages to be realty. These facts have made
available a method of taxation, which practically is impossible
in respect to many kinds of indebtedness.[4]

It would seem to be almost superfluous to argue that the
taxation of both land and mortgage is double taxation, were

---

[1] Knox *vs.* Com'rs (1878), 20 Kan., 596.

[2] Savings Bank *vs.* New London (1849), 20 Ct., 115 ; Branch *vs.* Town of Ma-
rengo (1876), 43 Ia., 600; Commw. *vs.* Peo. Sav. Bk. (1862), 87 Mass., 428;
Suffolk Bk., petr. (1889), 149 Mass., 1 ; People *vs.* Com'r Taxes (1874), 59 N. Y.,
40 ; Rosenberg *vs.* Weekes (1887), 67 Tex., 578.

[3] Story, *Conflict of Laws*, ch. xiv, §§ 424, 447, 543, 551, 591.

[4] The great importance of these debts is shown by the fact that the value, estimated in the last census, in thirty-three fairly representative states and territories, was $4,935,455,896, or 18.57 per cent. of all taxed real estate. In Penn-
sylvania the total was $613,105,802, or 18.91 per cent. of the true value of the
realty. *Cf. Report Penn. Tax Conference* (1894).

it not for the fact that it is frequently denied. Thus a well recognized tax commission in New Jersey asserted that such was not double taxation, on the ground of the separate nature of the land and the mortgage note. "Taxing each property once is not double taxation. The same is true in the transfer or sale of other things as well as of land. . . . The value of a credit is not dependent alone on the tangible things a debtor may own when the credit is made. It may be, and in fact usually is, dependent on his property of other descriptions, as well as on his honesty, industry and skill. The wealth of a civilized community does not consist merely of what can be seen and touched."[1] This only results, logically, in the advocacy of a system of taxation which shall include as taxable wealth, those invisible and intangible values, of "honesty, industry and skill." The Massachusetts Commission of 1875 attacked the theory from a similar point of view: "Most mortgages given for loans of money, or to secure the payment of debts, are drawn with promissory notes in the usual form, negotiable, and signed by the mortgagor. Such notes are parts of the mortgages, but are usually upon separate paper, and may be sued and collected separately. They have, aside from the security of the mortgaged land, an independent value, equal to that of the maker's ordinary note for the same amount. . . . The security of the mortgage may have become perfectly worthless . . . and yet the value of the mortgage, as property—the promise of a solvent debtor—be unimpaired. A land owner of abundant means may choose to mortgage, and actually be able to mortgage land again and again, until the security afforded by it would be utterly worthless."[2] This argument, apart from its disregard of general facts of mortgage debts; *i. e.*, that they are not usually loans of wealthy land-owners, and are not made a great many times on the same property—this argument, it is clear, only shifts the question to

[1] *N. J. Report*, 1868 (Ogden), quoted by *Mass. Report*, 1875 (Hills), p. 98.
[2] *Mass. Report*, 1875 (Hills), pp. 91–2.

general indebtedness, which, in the theoretical view advanced,
is the same as mortgage indebtedness.

The New York Commission of 1871 declared for the exemption of mortgages because it was impracticable to tax them.[1]
The Maryland Commission said it seemed "unfair" to exempt
the person deriving an income from mortgages, yet they
deemed it injudicious to repeal the law exempting them.[2]
They feared that the money lenders would refuse to extend
their loans to the farmers of the state.[3] It was also thought
that there was a kind of double taxation, resulting from the
taxation of both land and mortgage, not contemplated by the
Legislature when it exempted mortgages, *i. e.*, " it was always
shifted to the mortgagor, so'that he paid taxes, not only on
his land, but also on the money he borrowed on it."[4] That
the land should be taxed at its full value, and the taxes paid,
by " those who are logically if not legally co-proprietors of the
soil," has been strongly advocated as "the only rational system."[5]
The Committee of the Pennsylvania Tax Conference objected
to this on the ground that it would give rise to double taxation, owing to the fact that other states practiced a different
system.[6] The New York system allows the deduction of debts
from personal property. The counsel for the recent Tax Committee of the Legislature seemed to favor the idea of deductions from realty of mortgage debts, but did not propose it.[7]
The Tax Committee of the Legislature proposed to except
mortgages from the personal property from which debts might
be deducted.[8] This was in order to place it on the same footing as realty, and to prevent gross evasions of the revenue laws.

[1] *New York Report*, 1871, pp. 38–42.

[2] *Md. Tax Report*, 1888, p. 74.

[3] *Md. Tax Rept.*, 1888, p. 74.   [4] *Ibid.*, p. 76.

[5] Seligman, *Gen. Prop. Tax*, pp. 35, 36.

[6] *Penn. Tax Conf.*, 1894, *Committee Rept.*

[7] *Report of Counsel for N. Y. Tax Com.*, 1893, p. 14.

[8] *N. Y. Joint Com. on Tax*, 1893, p. 14.

Considering the demands of theory and practice, it seems that the most just method of taxation is, in general, that adopted by California and Massachusetts; tax the mortgagee on his interest and the mortgagor on the land minus the value of the mortgage. Further, adopt a rigid system of registration, and allow no contract between the parties to evade the law. The omission to require this last may easily make the whole system a farce.[1] The plausible argument that the exemption of the mortgage is a benefit to the mortgagor, since he receives a corresponding reduction in the rate of interest, is probably never completely true, sometimes very far from it.[2] This fact is well stated, as follows: " It is a mistake to suppose that, were the mortgage exempt in the hands of the holder, the owner of the land would thereby be relieved by a corresponding diminution of interest. The rate of interest upon mortgages depends upon many things more clearly than upon the rate of taxation. . . . In Connecticut the system of offsets does not give the borrower a lower rate than we enjoy."[3] The incidence of taxation is too intricate a problem, too much dependent upon particular facts of time and place, to be thus summarily settled. A correct system should be established without a too great solicitude concerning the competition of other states, who presumably are equally desirous of establishing a just system.[4]

In almost all the states, mortgages are taxed as personal property, and the mortgagors are allowed the same deductions for such debts as for unsecured indebtedness. Massachusetts, and California regard the interest of the mortgagor as an interest in the land, and taxable as such. Recently Michigan established the same method, but it was almost immediately abandoned. In Oregon also it was at one time the practice. In

---

[1] Seligman, *Gen. Prop. Tax*, p. 36.   [2] *Ibid.*
[3] *Mass. Rept.*, 1875, pp. 89–90.
[4] *Cf. Ohio Tax Com. Rept.*, 1893, p. 64.

Connecticut and New Jersey deductións are allowed from
property in land on account of mortgage indebtedness, but
this is limited by conditions as to the residence of the
mortgagees. In New York the mortgagor may deduct
his mortgage indebtedness from his personal property. In
Massachusetts and Connecticut, however, though the mortgage is taxable in the first instance, the mortgagor may contract to pay the taxes, and in New Jersey the mortgage is not
taxable unless a deduction is claimed. In Kansas a peculiar
provision exists in respect to the taxation of the mortgagee ;
he is not permitted to deduct his indebtedness therefrom as
from other credits. The mortgage in this respect is assimilated
to realty. In the judicial opinion respecting the taxation of
mortgages and the land without deduction, the courts have
generally held that it is not double taxation. Sometimes,
however, it has been declared not to be *unlawful* double taxation.[1] In Michigan, in a divided court, some of the justices
declared it to be unlawful double taxation.[2]

Corporation Bonds. The general principles of indebtedness
apply to the bonds of corporations as well as to the mortgage
debts of individuals. In some of their main features such
bonds are nothing more than mortgage debts, but in the character of the property hypothecated and in the methods of
transfer there are important differences. The peculiar nature
of such property has been not infrequently recognized in the
construction of the tax laws. To tax the entire property of a
corporation, a railroad, for example, and also the bondholders,
is evidently double taxation. If, however, the capital stock is
taxed instead of the property, this is avoided. The taxation
of bonds and shares reaches all the property of the corporation

---

[1] People *vs.* Worthington (1859), 21 Ill., 171; McGregor's Exr. *vs.* Vanpel
(1868), 24 Ia., 436; Insur. Co. *vs.* Lott (1875), 54 Ala., 499; App. of Fox and
Wife (1886), 112 Pa. St., 337.

[2] Peo. *vs.* Sanilac Supr., 71 Mich., 16.

without taxing any of it twice, and, of course, each should be taxed to the owner.

The theory has been advanced that, in general, the taxation of corporations upon all their property, and also the bond-holders on their bonds, is not double taxation. This depends upon the application of the principle of incidence called "capitalization." It has been asserted that, as a general rule, the tax operates to depreciate the value of the bonds, and that, consequently, subsequent purchasers get them at a discounted value, and hence are virtually free from taxation. Questions of incidence are, indeed, generally beyond the scope of this investigation, but so important and sweeping an application of the theories of incidence as would sanction such a great amount of *primâ facie* double taxation deserves attention. As Prof. Seligman says, the whole question depends upon whether the tax is general or partial : "For if the tax is general, there will be no depreciation in value. It is only when the tax is a partial tax, assessing some articles in the class more than others, that the tax will virtually be capitalized, and that a decrease of the value of the overtaxed article will ensue." An examination of the tax laws of the United States, and in fact of most countries, will show that not only are such bonds, or the income therefrom, generally taxable at the present time, but they have been for a long period. Even though the original holders have sold out, the present holders are truly paying a tax on their investment, simply because that form of investment has been taxed from the beginning, as well as most other great classes of values which would compete with it in the investment market.

The policies of the United States and the various states show great diversity in the treatment of the taxation of bonded debts and property. The income tax of the United States includes in its assessments the interest paid on bonds, but in the taxation of corporations only the net income of the corporation is taken, that is, the portion paid to shareholders or used

in further construction or investment. In the Virginia income
taxes the same principle is observed.

The typical form of taxation in the state systems is to tax
all the property of the corporation, as well as the bonds of the
bondholders. This, for example, is the practice in Alabama,
California, Georgia, Illinois, Iowa, Indiana, Louisiana, Ohio,
Tennessee, Texas, Virginia and Wisconsin. In some states the '
method is not quite so extreme. The bondholders are taxed,
but the corporation is taxed only on its tangible property and
the capital stock in excess thereof. Of course there may
be no capital stock in excess, and if there was a bonded debt
it would presumably make the actual worth of the corporation property as a means of income to the corporation of
less value than the tangible property. Examples of this
method are found in Kansas, Kentucky, Missouri and North
Carolina. In some of the states which tax all the property, as
well as the bonds of the bondholders, it is expressly provided
that the value of the corporate property shall be measured by
the aggregate values of the bonds and shares. This is the case
in California, Illinois and Tennessee. In California this is
especially notable, since for private mortgage indebtednes,
deduction is allowed from the property. That form of taxation
is conceded to be double taxation, and double taxation is contrary to its constitution, yet the courts held that corporations
could not claim the benefit of that provision.[1] In Illinois it is
frankly admitted that in a certain sense double taxation exists,
but not in any greater degree than is held legal in regard to
individuals, who are taxable in the same manner, without deduction of debts from property.[2]

The taxation of the bonds to the bondholders and the capital
stock to the corporation, does not produce double taxation.
Many states tax their corporations on capital stock, as for ex-

[1] C. P. Ry. Co. *vs.* Bd. Equal. (1882), 60 Cal., 35.

[2] Porter *vs.* Ry. Co. (1875), 76 Ill., 561.

ample Massachusetts, Michigan, Pennsylvania, and New York ; generally such taxes are not pure capital-stock taxes. Certain states, we have already shown, tax the tangible property plus the capital stock in excess thereof. Those states which tax the capital stock as a distinct corporation tax generally provide that the real estate shall be independently valued and taxed, and the value thereof deducted from the value of the capital stock. If the corporation had a very heavy debt, the value of the capital stock might be so small that the deduction of the value of the realty would leave nothing to be taxed. In the cases where bonded indebtedness exists, the realty is generally the important consideration, unless, indeed, there is a very valuable franchise or privilege. In Michigan, for example, the realty is deducted from the capital stock, and taxed separately; from the remaining value debts are deductible. This, though called a capital stock tax, is more strictly a property tax. Massachusetts also deducts the realty from the aggregate value of the shares. In New York there is no deduction of realty ; the total value of the capital stock is taxed.[1] In Pennsylvania the total capital stock is taxed.

Pennsylvania has, indeed, as far as is legally practicable, the ideal system, in regard to the taxation of corporations and their bondholders. A tax of a certain percentage is assessed on the value of the capital stock and also on the value of the bonds; both are paid by the corporation, but the tax on the bonds is deducted from the interest payments made to the bondholders. The total corporate property may be assessed in this way, and both parties taxed on their actual interest in the property. A somewhat similar method is practiced in Maryland. In Connecticut the corporations are taxed on the value of the stock and bonds; but the bondholder is exempt. Similarly in New Jersey the corporation is taxed on all the corporate property; if it claims a deduction for any indebted-

---

[1] Its realty is taxed independently, however.

ness, this is allowed in case the deduction so made can be collected from the creditor, *i. e.*, if the corporation demands a deduction for bonded indebtedness, it is allowed, in so far as the bondholders are taxable residents. The bondholders are not taxable unless such deduction is made.

Public Stock. In regard to public debts, it is plain there can arise no question of double taxation as far as they are concerned, for the property on which their solution depends is public property, and therefore not taxable. But looking at the matter as one of equal taxation, the possessors of such securities are as properly liable to taxation as though it were private indebtedness. If a contract exemption exists, of course, taxation cannot legitimately be demanded from the jurisdictions which granted the exemption. On other jurisdictions, however, no such obligation lies.

The federal form of the United States government gives rise to a peculiar condition in this respect. The doctrine of implied constitutional restrictions has been invoked to protect the obligations of the general government from taxation by the States, and in a more feeble manner the bonds of the several States have been held exempt, on the same grounds, from Federal taxation. The bonds issued by the United States have been declared exempt from taxation on their face, and this exemption is formally recognized in the income tax law. The states have never been permitted to tax them.[1] But, in regard to the indirect taxation of such securities, the position of the Supreme Court has been much less rigorous. At first, even this was denied, but now it has been established that no deduction need be made for the possession of such property, either in the taxation of national bank shares,[2] the assessment of the capital stock of a corporation,[3] the taxation of the

---

[1] Weston *vs.* Charleston, 2 Peters, 449.

[2] Van Allen *vs.* Assess. (1865), 3 Wall., 273.

[3] Home Ins. Co. *vs.* State (1890), 134 U. S., 594.

deposits of savings banks,[1] or the assessment of the property and franchise of a corporation.[2]

The immunity from federal taxation of obligations issued by the state has not been consistently recognized in the direct taxes levied by Congress; but, in the recent income tax decision, the Supreme Court has held it to be unconstitutional. The several states, however, are not restrained by any constitutional requirement from taxing each other's obligations.[3]

The tax laws of the states generally provide that all public stocks shall be taxed; exemptions may exist, though not specified in the tax laws, if it has been so contracted. There appears to be no rule as to the taxation of stock which the state itself has issued. In Alabama, New Jersey, North Carolina and Pennsylvania, for example, the stock issued by the state is expressly declared to be exempt. On the other hand, in California, Connecticut, Iowa, Ohio, Tennessee, Virginia and Maryland, such securities are declared taxable.[4] In Georgia the court decided that such bonds were not intended to be taxed, though it did not decide the legality of such taxation.[5] The state courts have also often declared the taxation of United States bonds unconstitutional; in a Maryland case, it was placed upon the ground that such property was not a part of the resources of the state.[6] Owing to the exemption of certain kinds of public stock, especially United States bonds, provision has been made in some states for the prevention of an evasive investment therein, for the purpose of escaping taxation. Debts are not deductible from exempt securities in New York. In Alabama such bonds are taxable, if converted

---

[1] Prov. Inst. *vs.* Mass. (1867), 6 Wall., 611.

[2] State Ry. Tax Cases (1875), 92 U. S., 575.

[3] Bonaparte *vs.* Tax Court (1888), 104 U. S., 592.

[4] *Cf.* Champaigne Co. Bk. *vs.* Smith (1857), 7 O. St., 42 ; Comr. *vs.* Maury (1887), 82 Va., 883.

[5] Miller *vs.* Wilson (1878), 60 Ga., 505.

[6] Howell *vs.* State (1845), 3 Gill, 14.

during a certain period. In Kansas a special method of assessment is provided; the number of months for which such stock is held is divided into the value thereof, and the quotient is multiplied by the number of months in the year remaining, and that product is listed and taxed as moneys. This has been approved by the United States Supreme Court.[1]

Though United States securities may not be taxed as property, the income therefrom is not exempt. Such income is taxable in Virginia. In Kentucky an attempt was made to tax the income, under a special provision, at a rate which practically amounted to a property tax; but the court held that it was a colorable evasion.[2]

Shares. This species of property has been included with debts, in this discussion, as a *quasi* debt,[3] though in the best legal view it is quite distinct. In an economic sense, shares possess in a marked degree those characteristics of debts which are important in this connection. In the first place, they derive their value from the fact that they represent the claim of one person on the property of another. The usual form of debt is the claim for a specific sum of money; but it may also be for a specific annual interest payment, *etc.* In a similar way, a share is a claim for a contingent dividend payment, and also on the dissolution of the corporation for a certain portion of the property. Debts have usually been treated almost as if they had independent property value, and this was also to a certain extent the view in respect to shares. Now, however, shares are commonly conceded to represent an undivided interest in the corporate property, though most debts are still treated as distinct and separate from the property on which their payment and their value depends. The reasons for this are quite obvious. In the case of the debtor and creditor, we

---

[1] Mitchell *vs.* Com'rs., 1 Otto. 206.

[2] Bank of Ky. *vs.* Commw. (1872), 9 Bush, 47.

[3] This term is used in Tax Collector *vs.* Insur. Co., 42 La. An., 1172.

have two persons whose property interests are as separate and distinct as their physical existence; in the case of the corporation shareholder, however, we find a mingling; the interests are almost identical, the shareholder is himself a component of the corporate person, and his dividends a portion of the net income of the corporation.

Viewing the property in shares in this light, it is quite evi-dent that to tax them, and at the same time to tax the corporation on its property, or in any other manner which may take the place of a property tax, such as a tax on capital stock or earnings, can not be considered otherwise than as double tax-ation of the most positive sort. It is hardly necessary to state that the resources which pay the taxes in either case must be considered economically to be the same in both cases, and that what the corporation pays, as such, must be to the same extent a loss to the shareholders severally. The circumstances, if another illustration be deemed not superfluous, are really the same, in this respect, as that of a private partnership. No one would assert that a partnership should be taxed on its property in the name of the firm, and that each partner should also be liable individually for what he had already paid taxes on, jointly with his associates.

Does the question of incidence intervene to alter our conclusions on this point? Evidently the same argument can be advanced here as in the case of bonded indebtedness. Whether the taxes on shares of stock are capitalized, so that the subsequent holders practically escape by discounting it, will depend upon the character of the general taxation of property. If the property tax is general, in fact as well as theory, there will be no capitalization. Where corporations are not taxed on property, but according to special methods, the tax so assessed against them is, however, merely an equivalent for the property tax, and, broadly speaking, it is immaterial whether they come under one method of assessment or the other. The faults of our state tax systems do not consist in not taxing all

property, but in attempting to tax it twice. Suppose, however, that the tax is capitalized, that does not justify the taxation of the shareholder.

We have considered this question of the taxation of the
shareholder and the corporation on the supposition that the
shareholder is an individual. If, however, the shareholder is
also a corporation, even though shares themselves are not
directly taxable, the investment of corporations in such property, with a system of taxation on capital stock, would involve
double taxation. The shares, of course, should be deducted
from the value of the stock.[1]

The almost universal practice in this country is to exempt
the shares of stock to the stockholder, if the corporation is taxable on its stock or property. In some states property and
shares are both taxable to some extent without causing double
taxation; first, in case the shares are taxed, all property not
included in the value of the shares may be taxed also; and,
second, where the property is originally taxed, all value of the
shares in excess of the assessed value of the property may be
also taxed. These provisions are just, at least so far as the
question of property and shares is concerned. Only a few
states allow the taxation of property to the corporation and
shares to the shareholder. North Carolina permits this form
of double taxation, and also Wyoming. Apparently shares of
corporations are taxable in Virginia, although the property is
likewise taxed. Shares are taxable in Iowa, whether the corporation is taxed upon its property or not, except in the case
of manufacturing corporations. In thirty-five States, however,
this kind of double taxation has been expressly prohibited by
statute. The United States income tax law makes a similar
provision in declaring that the dividends of corporations which
are taxed upon their income shall not be taxed to the share-

---

[1] An astonishing case of quadruple taxation as a result of such a method of taxation is given in the preliminary report of the Pennsylvania Tax Conference on
the "Valuation and Taxation of Railroads in Pennsylvania," p. 17.

holders receiving them. A like exemption exists under the Virginia income tax law.

Generally corporations, with the exception of banks, are taxable upon their property or capital stock, or in some equivalent manner, so that the individual is not taxed upon his shares. Sometimes, however, the shareholders are taxed and the corporation is exempt. The Massachusetts tax on corporate franchise may be viewed more correctly, perhaps, as a tax on the shareholders than on the corporation. The tax is assessed in the aggregate to the corporation, it is true, but, with the exception of the shares of non-residents, the amounts assessed to the shareholders are credited in due proportion, for local taxation, to the place where the shareholder resides. In Maryland the tax is assessed against the shareholders, and the amount due is deducted by the officers of the corporation from the dividends. In both Massachusetts and Maryland the realty is taxed at its actual *situs*, but the value so assessed is deducted from the aggregate value of the shares, and the remainder, in the proportion of their shares, is taxed to the shareholders. In Vermont a method prevails somewhat similar to that in Massachusetts. The shares are listed and taxed to the individual. The non-residents' shares in domestic corporations are taxed by means of a deduction from his dividends. From the actual value of the shares all realty which is taxed is deducted, and, in the case of the manufacturing corporations, all personalty which has been otherwise taxed. Connecticut taxes a few corporations in this way, and, until recently, all Louisiana corporations were taxed in the same manner.

Special methods are generally provided for the taxation of banks. This is due to the requirements of the Federal law that national banks located in states shall be taxable only on their shares and real estate. It is required that the shareholders shall be assessed on the shares, and not the corporation, and that the rate of taxation shall not be greater than that on other moneyed capital. The states have been careful to observe these restrictions, and generally have taxed their own banks, and sometimes similar moneyed insititutions, in the same manner.

The judicial decisions are far from unanimous in declaring the taxation of shares and property to be double taxation, or in disallowing it. This may be explained, apart from the conservatism of most courts, to the fact that the older decisions often represent a period of financial development now passed, when the statutes also may have expressly required such double taxation. The primary legal question is, of course, as to the identity of shares and corporate property. In the leading case of Van Allen *vs.* Assessors [1] the United States Supreme Court denied their identity. This has been frequently confirmed. On the other hand, recent decisions have pronounced the contrary view. [2] Sometimes the courts have declared that such taxation is not not double taxation. [3] Again they have admitted that double taxation existed, but have held that it was within the legislative power. [4] They have very frequently held that it is double taxation, and unlawful. [5] In the same State there are often found decisions on both sides of the case, as, for example, in Iowa, Kentucky, Indiana, Ohio, Pennsylvania and New Jersey. But the general tenor of judicial opinion appears to be against such taxation in most States,

[1] Van Allen *vs.* Assess. (1865), 3 Wall., 573.

[2] State of Tenn. *vs.* Bk. of Commerce (1893,) 53 Fed. R., 735; San Francisco *vs.* Mackay (1884), 21 Fed. R., 539.

[3] Danville Bk. Co. *vs.* Parks (1878), 88 Ill., 170; St. Ry. Co. *vs.* Morrow (1888), 3 Pickle (Tenn.), 406; Lee *vs.* Sturges (1889), 46 O. St., 153.

[4] *Cf.* Conwell *vs.* Connersville (1860), 15 Ind., 150; Cook *vs.* Burlington (1882), 59 Ia., 251; Whitesell *vs.* Northampton Co. (1865), 49 Pa. St., 526; State *vs.* Collector (1874), 8 Vr. (N. J.), 258.

[5] Vallee *vs.* Zeigler (1884), 84 Mo., 214; State *vs.* Haight (1884), 2 Vr. (N. J.), 399; Tallman *vs.* Treas. (1861), 12 Ia., 531; R. R. Co. *vs.* Barbour (1888), 88 Ky., 73; Hoadley *vs.* Essex Com'rs. (1870), 105 Mass., 519; McIver *vs.* Robinson (1875), 53 Ala., 456; Burke *vs.* Badlam (1881), 57 Cal., 594; Jones *vs.* Davis (1880), 35 O. St., 474; Gillespie *vs.* Gaston (1887), 67 Tex., 599.

viz., Alabama, California, Illinois, Iowa, Kansas, Kentucky, Louisiana, Massachusetts, Maine, Minnesota, Missouri, New Jersey, Ohio and Texas. The opposite view appears to be approved in North Carolina, Pennsylvania and Tennessee.

CHAPTER IV.

PROPERTY AND INCOME.

THE taxation of property and income does not itself predicate double taxation. Accepting broadly the principle that income is the criterion of ability, it follows that a general income tax is in itself complete. Property taxes do not reach all sources of income. Hence, if both property and income taxes exist together, so much of the income as is derived from taxable property should be exempt, or else the income which is not derived from property should be taxed twice. In the latter case there would be no double taxation, but repetition merely. The only difficulty here is in determining to what extent property may be considered the source of income. Where property is used in business the income does not necessarily depend on the property alone. Special income taxes may be levied in addition to a property tax, therefore, without producing double taxation or inequality, if the incomes of property are not also taxed. With a general income tax, however, the addition of special income taxes would always produce double taxation.

There are some special taxes which vary considerably in their methods of assessment and rating, but which sometimes take the form of income taxes. Such are certain taxes on privileges and occupations. Often these are aimed at sources of income not affected by property taxes. They may be quite free, therefore, from the imputation of double taxation. Often they have the appearance of license taxes. Sometimes difficulties are experienced in clearly discriminating income taxes from property taxes. Where certain kinds of property are exempt the income therefrom may be taxed, and according to the rate such income is taxed, it may be classed as an income or a property tax.   On the other hand, income, as sometimes in the case of gross receipts, may be taxed as property or accrued income.

For convenience of treatment we may distinguish, among income taxes, the following kinds, *viz.*: income in general, income from particular kinds of business, income from privileged callings, and income from special kinds of property.

General Income.   A tax levied on all incomes is, in itself, an equitable form of taxation.   If, however, a general property tax also exists, it is clear that those deriving income from property will be doubly taxed, since the property tax is not itself universal; that is, it does not reach service incomes.   Therefore the incomes from property in such a case should be exempt.   But, in perhaps a large proportion of cases, income is mixed in its derivation; it is partly the interest of capital, partly the profits or wages of the owner for his management thereof.   With respect to many forms of property no confusion is likely to arise on this account.   For example, in the taxation of a house, no account need be taken of anything but its rental value.   A tax on the property would exhaust its liability.   When the stock of goods of a merchant is considered, it is evident that the taxation of such property at its value does not gauge the real ability of the merchant.   His capitalized income will seldom correspond to the value of the stock of goods.   It may be more, it may be less.   Taking the stock of goods to mean the average amount on hand—and this seems to be the fairest way—it is evident that there is no necessary connection between its value and the income of the merchant. Three important factors enter which are variables; the first is the amount of credit capital employed, which tends to enlarge the value of the stock as compared with the income; the second is the rate of conversion, which tends to enlarge the income as compared with the stock value; the third is the rate of profit on the sales, and thus will have the same effect as the first and second, according as the rate of profit is low or high respectively. Of course there is generally some compensatory relation between high profits on sales and slow conversions, and *vice versâ*. Suppose that the merchant is taxed on his capital invested, *i. e.*, the value which under fair conditions he could withdraw from the business ; in this case the uncertainties as to what the stock is and as to what deductions should be made are obviated. It is doubtless true that even this value does not normally equal the capitalized value of the income which the merchant would derive from such an investment in his business, because it takes no account of gains due to his own management and labor. So the taxation of the capital employed in such business and also of the income to a certain extent, would not involve double taxation.

General income taxes are very infrequent in this country in the tax systems of the states. There are only three examples of any consequence : the income taxes of the United States, Massachusetts and Virginia. The Virginia income tax is general, and is assessed in addition to a general tax on property, so that incomes derived from property are taxed twice. In Massachusetts the tax is assessed only against those incomes which are not derived from property subject to taxation. Under this law a celebrated decision was made, in which the court attempted to distinguish between income derived from property and the profits of business.[1] The court held that the income derived from trade in merchandise, which was taxed as stock in trade, was not " derived from property subject to taxation." The court said : " The income from a profession, trade or employment, which is taxable under our system of laws, is an entirely different thing from the capital invested in the business, or the stock of goods in the purchase of which the whole or part of such capital may have been expended. The income meant by the statute is the income for the year, and is

---

[1] Wilcox *vs.* Com'rs (1870), 103 Mass., 544.

the result of the year's business. It is the net result of many
combined influences; the use of the capital invested; the personal labor and services of the members of the firm; the skill
and ability with which they lay in or from time to time renew
their stock ; the carefulness and good judgment with which
they sell and give credit, and the foresight and address with
which they hold themselves prepared for the fluctuations and
contingencies affecting the general commerce and business of
the country. To express it in a more summary and compre-
hensive form, it is the creation of capital, industry and skill."

There is much merit in this opinion, but it goes too far. Undoubtedly the profits of the firm were due to the skill and
industry of the members, but all property must be used and
managed to yield any returns. If they had not exercised foresight they would not only have failed to obtain profits, but
they would presumably have lost some, perhaps all, of their
property. Suppose, instead of merchants' stock, their capital
had been invested in a hotel. To say in that case that the income was not derived partly from property would be absurd.
When the court said that income was taxable which was
derived from " industry and skill," it was right; but when it
added thereto " capital," it was denying all meaning and sense
to the statutory clause that " no income shall be taxed which
is derived from property subject to taxation; for capital is
property, and the income ' created ' by capital and the income
' derived ' from property are the same." [1]

[1] The following defense was made of the Massachusetts income tax : " The
conclusions which withhold us from recommending its defeat are that without it
many inhabitants of ability would escape direct taxation, and many others would
contribute, not in proportion to ability, but to property in possession only, and that,
properly construed and uniformly and thoroughly administered, it works no injustice, but perfects our system, and insures that every inhabitant ' shall contribute
proportionably to his ability to all common charges.' . . . The ability derived
from mere property is no greater in the hands of one than another. Bank stock
held by the greatest merchant yields no more dividend than if in the estate of an
infant or lunatic. . . . But the gains of the merchant, or trader, or manufacturer,

Income from Particular Businesses. The taxation of the income of certain kinds of business is very common in the United States. The usual form is the taxation of the net or gross receipts or earnings of transportation, telegraph and other companies, and the premiums of insurance companies. Sometimes these taxes are in lieu of property taxes, and in that case the presumption is that no double taxation exists. But they are often levied in addition to the property taxes, and then, from the fact that other corporations of not dissimilar character are not also taxed, it would seem that double taxation arises. But it must be borne in mind that in the case of some of these companies the property of the corporation forms a totally inadequate measure of its real ability. This is a fact with a great many corporations, but is very conspicuously so, for example, in the case of express companies.[1] Gross receipts

are not of the same nature as the interest of money, or the dividends of stock, or the yield of land, or rent of buildings. The gain is due to the skill of the man, rather than to the property to which he may apply it, and is an ability of which, for purposes of taxation, the gain or income is a fair measure. Still less can receipts from mere salaries or from professional employment be compared, in this respect, with dividends, or interest money, or rents, from property once taxed."
—*Mass. Tax Rept.,* 1875, pp. 51-53.

[1] The recent Ohio Tax Commission used the following language : " In a modern community there are aggregations of persons, sometimes enjoying corporate franchises and sometimes not incorporated, who are the recipients of large revenues drawn from the mass of the people's earnings, and who yet own little or no tangible property. Instances will readily occur to every one. An express company may own nothing within the State beyond a few horses and wagons and trucks ; a telephone company or telegraph company owns a few miles of wire, which is worthless except as a source of revenue, and a number of instruments of small value. . . . It is apparent that in all of these cases the property owned is no index whatever of the ability to aid in bearing the burdens of the State . . . it should be determined by earnings, not by property." In view of this condition of affairs this Commission proposed the following remedy : " It is suggested that the deficiency which exists be supplemented by a franchise tax upon the privilege of exercising its corporate franchises or of carrying on its business in a corporate capacity in the State ; this franchise tax may properly be a percentage based upon the gross earnings within the State."—*Ohio Tax Com.,* 1893, pp. 48, 60.

taxes, in addition to a property tax, may often have the same justification as general income taxes in addition to a property tax. They reach sources of wealth not fairly represented by property. A distinction should be made between the taxation of gross receipts and property, and gross receipts and capital stock. Take for example an express company. Its capital stock may have a considerable value, far exceeding its tangible property, and truly representing its earning capacity. While a tax on gross receipts and property might give rise to no injustice, a tax on gross receipts and capital stock might really be unequal, unless other corporations were subjected to equivalent burdens. So also with insurance companies; their real and personal property situated in a state does not represent the taxable value of their business therein.[1]

Taxes on the incomes of special kinds of business go under a variety of names; they are generally termed taxes on incomes, receipts, earnings or premiums, and they may be levied on the gross or the net return. Their legal classification is various; often, to avoid legal or constitutional objections, they are called licenses, or excises, or assessments of the corporate franchise, or taxes on the privilege of doing business. These distinctions have generally no economic validity.

Taxes on receipts or income are usually upon the gross sum. The rate of taxation is almost always declared in the statute, while the rate of property assessments, and also, generally, of the capital stock, is fixed by apportionment. The relation between the net and gross return is of course very different in different classes of business, and therefore, the rate of assessment is properly differentiated, in order that approximately equal results may be attained on the net returns. In the same kind of business, moreover, the relation of the gross receipts to profits is quite different in one state from another. Where the concentration of business is great, the same amount of gross receipts represents a much greater profit, so that as

---

[1] *Cf. Rept. Maine Tax Com.*, 1890, p. 68.

between different states the rates of assessment should be different in the same kind of business. The extent to which such variations exist in different kinds of business is not the same. For example, it may be generally asserted first, that there is a much greater difference between gross and net receipts in railroad than in express companies; second, that as to railroad companies a greater difference between gross and net receipts will be found in sparsely settled regions than in densely populated districts; and third, that these latter variations will be much more important with railways than with express companies.

New York and Pennsylvania tax all railroad, transportation, telegraph and telephone companies, both on their capital stock and their gross receipts. The gross receipts taxes are additional. In Michigan, on the contrary, where railroads are taxed primarily on their receipts, the property and capital stock are exempt. The receipts tax on Michigan railways is a classified or graduated tax ranging from 2 per cent. to 4 per cent. The system in Maine is similar; railroads are taxed according to the gross receipts per mile, in about a dozen classes, the rates ranging from one-fourth to three and one-fourth per cent. The realty and fixtures outside of the road itself are also taxable. In Vermont, in the taxation of railways, an alternative property or gross earnings tax is provided. In Minnesota certain railways are taxable on gross receipts in lieu of all other taxation. In Wisconsin, also, railways are subject to a graded receipts tax in lieu of property taxation. In North Carolina, only such railways as are not taxed on their capital are taxed on receipts. Gross receipts and property are taxed to telegraph, telephone and express companies in North Carolina, to express companies in Missouri, to telegraph, telephone and railway companies in Virginia, and to gas, water, electric light and various other companies in Alabama. In Virginia, however, the gross receipts taxes are part of a general income tax system. On the other hand, where gross receipts are taxed, the property is exempt in the taxation of express and telegraph companies in Georgia and Vermont, the car companies of Vermont and Michigan, and the telegraph companies of Wisconsin.

The same diversity of practice is found in the taxation of insurance companies. In New York, Pennsylvania and North Carolina they are taxed on their premiums and also on their capital stock, and in Texas, Virginia, Alabama, Iowa, *etc.*, they are taxed on their premiums and property. On the other hand, the property of insurance companies which are taxed on their premiums is exempt in some states, as, for example, in Ohio, Tennessee, Wisconsin and Georgia. In Pennsylvania the net earnings of private bankers and brokers are taxed as well as their real and personal property. In Massachusetts certain corporations organized to do business outside of the state, and holding most of their property abroad, are taxed on their net profits.

The courts have seldom considered the justice of these taxes, since there has been little question but that they are within the scope of legislative authority. In Iowa, where under a former law both the property and the receipts of an express company were taxed, the court held that though it might be unequal and unjust, it was not invalid.[1]

Income from Privilege and Occupation. It is not easy to distinguish the taxes on privilege here included from many other taxes which are frequently assessed on the privilege of doing business, which have been already considered. There is, nevertheless, in general a plain economic division, which may be described as follows: The taxes on gross receipts, premiums and other taxes of a similar character, which we have treated above, are generally levied on corporations, or upon companies which do a business commonly undertaken by corporations, and particularly such as do an inter-state business; the taxes on privileges and occupations, on the other

[1] U. S. Exp. Co. *vs.* Ellyson (1869), 28 Ia., 370.

hand, may or may not be on the same legal footing, but, in either case, they are generally on individuals and the property affected is of a local character. One reason for the gross receipts taxes on great corporations doing an inter-state business is that they can be effectively taxed in that manner where a property tax would be of little consequence. Occupation taxes seem to stand also for the taxation of incomes which are only to a small extent derived from property, but they are aimed at the income of local business, and have a strong resemblance to license taxes. Although, therefore, in these methods of taxing the revenue of business, there is no clearly defined division, yet, theoretically as well as practically, the general distinction is at once recognized as legitimate and useful.

The taxes on gross receipts are found all over the United States. Taxes on privilege or occupation for state purposes, however, are almost entirely limited to the southern states. In the northern and northwestern states they rarely occur, except for local purposes. State privilege taxes are generally supplementary to the general *ad valorem* taxation of property. Thus in Virginia, Louisiana and Tennessee, where very extensive systems of privilege taxes exist, property taxes are also levied, and in Virginia a general income tax besides. It is not to be presumed on this account that double taxation is necessarily involved, because the very purpose of these taxes is evidently to reach ability not adequately taxed by the *ad valorem* tax. In Missouri the privilege tax levied on merchants is in lieu of property taxation. The rates are generally specified for each particular occupation or business. Not all of these taxes take the form of income taxes. Most of those that are rated according to income do not follow it in strict proportion. The more common method is to classify the income in fixed groups, with either a percentage or a specific tax on each group. The most various methods may be found in Louisiana, Virginia, Tennessee, Texas and Florida.

§ 5. *Income from Particular Kinds of Property.* It is some-times found that the income of certain kinds of property is tax-able, especially if the property from which the income flows is itself exempt. There are two kinds; natural products of cer-tain exempt lands, *etc.*, as crops or ores, and the income of in-tangible property, such as bonds, stocks and annuities. It is doubtful often whether these taxes, though in appearance in-come taxes, are not often, in fact, property taxes. The rate on an income basis should be ten times or more, that lev-ied on property; if, therefore, it is found that the rate as-sessed on such produce or income is approximately a property rate, then, undoubtedly, such a tax must be considered a prop-erty tax. An example of this kind of taxation is found in North Carolina, where the income from property not taxed is subject to a tax of five per cent. In Kentucky a similar tax on United States bonds was held unlawful.[1]

[1] Bk. of Ky. *vs.* Com. (1872), 9 Bush, 47.

CHAPTER V.

PROPERTY, CAPITAL STOCK AND SPECIFIC TAXES.

THIS chapter includes those forms of double taxation which occur through the taxation of property *eo nomine*, and also indirectly by taxes on capital stock, franchises and privileges. These are found chiefly in connection with corporations, though privilege taxes are often assessed to individuals. The economic identity which exists to a greater or less degree between capital stock and property is obvious. The term "franchise tax," as commonly applied to corporation taxation, has no necessary relation to any actual franchise or privilege which the corporation may possess; it is a convenient phrase used to avoid certain constitutional limitations which are commonly connected with property taxes. It gives rise to double taxation in case it is really in substance an additional important tax on property. These "franchise taxes" are levied on various principles. As they are not generally taxes on franchise, economically viewed, they may be termed "excises" for convenience of distinction. We may then distinguish three important kinds of taxes to be here considered, *viz.*, capital stock, excise, and privilege taxes.

Capital Stock. Capital stock taxes are of various kinds; the value assessed may be the par, market or actual value. In every case it is evident that between the capital stock and the property there exists a virtual identity of values, of a greater or less extent, which under some conditions is practically complete.[1] The capital stock may sometimes represent more than

---

[1] *Cf.* Seligman, *Taxation of Corp., op. cit.*, p. 642.

the tangible property; its value may be largely based on valuable franchises, patents, *etc.* On the other hand, the tangible property values may exceed the value of the capital stock, if the corporation is in debt. Now it will scarcely be found that both capital stock at its full value and all the property of a corporation are taxed under any system, even where their real identity is denied through some legal distinction. But in the methods of assessment of property and capital stock, and the deductions allowed on account of values taxed under one method or the other, considerable divergence will be found, and various degrees of partial double taxation. Moreover, it is not sufficient that all the property of the corporation should be taxed, and that it should be taxed only once, but, also, it should be taxed to the true economic owners *i. e.*, the problem of indebtedness must be taken into account in taxing corporations. The question of the taxation of indebtedness of corporations to their creditors has been considered already; it is sufficient to notice here whether deduction for such indebtedness is allowed. We must briefly notice here a question of inter-state complications, which will receive more detailed consideration later. It is impolitic for the states to allow an unlimited deduction for indebtedness, such as will reduce the amount of taxable tangible property; because, if the creditor is a non-resident and beyond the jurisdiction of the state, it is impossible under the present legal conditions to tax him instead of the debtor corporation. It is deemed more expedient that property should be taxed twice than that the state should not reach it at all.

Generally capital stock is taxed like property by apportionment and valuation, but in some cases a specific rate is fixed by the statute. This evidently affects the problem of double taxation only as a matter of detail, *i. e.*, the accuracy or justness of the particular rate which is so substituted. If the tax is assessed on the par value of stock, the tax assessment assumes an arbitrary and inelastic character which generally results in inequality. The most common method of assessing capital stock and property is as follows: The realty and tangible personalty are taxed under the methods of the general property tax, and this value is deducted from the assessed value of the capital stock, and the remainder is taxed (in addition to the property) under the name of capital stock. This method is practiced for example in North Carolina, Kansas, Georgia, Kentucky, Indiana and Alabama. It has one evident defect. If the capital stock is less in value than the tangible property, there is no reduction allowed on the assessment of the property. Many corporations have large property possessions whose capital stock is of little value; the bondholders are the real owners of the property, and on them should fall the burden of taxation to the extent of their interest. Further, it may be observed that this taxation of tangible property does not include the franchise values, which in many cases are of first importance; at least the franchise would not be included except under special principles of assessment.[1] In case the franchise is not included, and the value of the tangible property exceeds the value of the capital stock, then, unless the franchise value is reached (as it ought to be in such a case) by the taxation of the bondholders, it will escape entirely. In Indiana provision has been made for this contingency; "in all cases where the franchise is of greater value than the capital stock, then the franchise shall be assessed at its full cash value, and the capital stock in such case shall not be assessed."[2] Similar to the above method of assessment is that which is practiced in Massachusetts, Michigan, in the local taxation of

---

[1] In the taxation of railroad property, however, where the question of franchise value is, perhaps, of the greatest importance, an exception to this statement is quite often found. It is a well-recognized principle in the assessment of such property as a railroad track, bed and right of way, that the direct items of present cost, such as lands, ties, rails, *etc.*, are not the principal items of value, but rather its quality as a part of a continuous railroad having valuable traffic.

[2] *Ind. Acts*, 1891, 6 Mar., §§ 73, 74.

New York and elsewhere, in which realty only is deducted from the capital stock valuation. In New York this method is used for local taxation principally, another capital stock tax being used for state purposes.

The second principal method of taxing capital stock is based on the value of both stock and bonds. Illustrations of this are found in the laws of Illinois, California and Tennessee. The object in this method is to reach all the property of a corporation, whether tangible or intangible, regardless of its indebtedness. It is evident that there can be no values not represented in the value of the stock and bonds. This tax is levied entirely on the corporation, without regard to the bondholder, the valuation of the bonds, as well as the stock, being merely a method of arriving at the true value of the property and franchise. The tangible property in Illinois and California is separately assessed and taxed, and the value deducted from the aggregate value of stock and bonds, and the remainder so found is taxed as the value of the franchise. The only adverse criticism of this method of taxation is that no allowance is made for indebtedness.[1] In Connecticut a similar method is practiced, though with very important modifications. The tangible property is not valued at all, but the aggregate of the shares of stock and the aggregate of the bonds are taxed at a value fixed by certain special regulations, at a specific rate of one per cent.; this is in lieu of all other taxes, not only on the

---

[1] It has been frequently stated that the total value of the corporate property is represented by the value of the bonds plus the stock. On general principles this seems clear enough. In the taxation of railroads, however, it has been claimed that it was not just to take the sum of the stock and the actual value of the bonds, because the latter often had an excessive, fictitious value. That is, the road was not actually worth the sum represented thereby. This is accounted for by the fact that one railroad sometimes guarantees the interest payments of another. " Some of the bonds of many railroads would be actually worthless were it not for this guarantee." It was therefore proposed that the par value of the bonds be substituted (in case they did not fall below par). The conclusions seem faulty in some respects, and of course such conditions are rather exceptional.— *Cf. Report Penn. Tax Conference.*

property, but also on the shares and bonds. The taxation of
all the property without duplication is accomplished by this
method, but it disregards the principle of indebtedness.

New York has a special method of taxing capital stock for
State purposes, which is as follows: If the dividends equal or
exceed 6 per cent., the tax is $\frac{1}{4}$ of a mill upon the capital
stock for each per centum of the dividend; if the dividends are
less than 6 per cent., then 1 $\frac{1}{2}$ mills on each dollar of the value
of the stock; $i.\ e.$, the capital stock is valued according to
the dividends. The realty of the corporation is also taxable
without any deduction on account thereof. As the value of
the stock may largely be derived from the real estate, this is
patently double taxation. The method was borrowed from
Pennsylvania, but that state has recently discarded it, because
the burden was thought to be unequally great on those corporations declaring less than 6 per cent. dividends. Instead
thereof a tax on the capital stock of five mills on the dollar
has been substituted. This tax is for state purposes only, and
is in lieu of all other taxation. It is important to note that in
Pennsylvania an attempt was formerly made to tax the corporations and their bondholders directly for their respective interests in the corporate property within the state. The capital
stock was taxed to the corporation, and the bonds were taxed
to the bondholders where the road was situated, by means of
deductions made from the interest payments. While this
system was perfectly correct from an economic standpoint, the
United States Supreme Court declared that it was unlawful to
tax the non-resident bondholders in that manner, and, although
the tax on the resident bondholders continues to be assessed
as before, the method has been emasculated by this limitation.
The consideration of this subject, however, belongs to the second part of the question—the discussion of jurisdiction.

Generally it has been held that a tax on the capital stock of
a corporation is a tax on the property, in the legal as well as
the practical view of the question. This is the case, for exam-

ple, in Alabama, Connecticut, Indiana, Missouri, North Carolina, Ohio and Pennsylvania. In Indiana the court said, "a tax assessed upon the capital stock of a corporation is a tax upon the property of which the capital stock is composed;"[1] again, in Missouri, the court said, "if the stock and the property it represents are both taxed, the taxation is double;"[2] so also in Pennsylvania a tax upon the capital stock of a corporation is declared to be "a tax upon its property and assets."[3] In fact it may be expected that the courts will veto any attempt to tax both the entire property and capital stock as double taxation. On the other hand, and for different reasons, it has sometimes been denied that a tax on capital stock was a tax on property. The purpose of the courts in such cases has been to permit certain methods of taxation which were not considered inequitable in themselves, but which, if held to be property taxes, would be contrary to some constitutional provision or some principle of jurisprudence. Thus, the tax on capital stock in New York has been declared to be a tax on the corporate franchise or business.[4] In Massachusetts the courts were reduced to the extremity of declaring a tax on the aggregate shares of stock (from which a deduction of taxable realty was provided) an "excise" upon a "commodity." "The tax," said the court, "cannot be held valid, unless it can be construed to be in the nature of an excise on the franchise. . . . It certainly cannot be contended that the legislature can legitimately impose a tax upon property in the name or under the guise of an excise or duty. Such legislation would be palpable evasion."[5] Economically and practically the tax was, in every sense of the word, a tax on property; it was levied in a

---

[1] Whitney *vs.* City (1864), 23 Ind., 331.

[2] Hannibal Ry. Co. *vs.* Shacklett (1860), 30 Mo., 550.

[3] Commw. *vs.* Stand. Oil Co. (1882), 101 Pa. St., 119.

[4] Peo. *vs.* Home Ins. Co. (1883), 92 N. Y., 328; aff'd in Home Ins. Co. *vs.* State (1890), 134 U. S., 594.

[5] Commw. *vs.* Hamilton Mfg. Co. (1866), 94 Mass., 298.

peculiar manner in order to include the shares of non-residents, though much simpler means were available.

Property and Excise. Under this title are included those taxes on corporations and companies taxed like corporations, in which some of the property connected with their business may be used as a varying standard of assessment, as, for example, the policies of an insurance company, yet such property is not taxed as a distinct kind of property, but is used as a standard only; or in which the criterion is some purely physical quality, as the mileage of telegraph wire, or the number of tons of ore mined ; or in which some other arbitrary measure is used, as the number of telegraph messages ; or the tax may be fixed at a lump sum, *etc.*

These taxes are usually called franchise taxes, a term applied also to taxes on capital stock and various forms of income taxes.   It is not a tax on the franchise in an economic sense, any more than they are.   That term cannot be used, therefore, either to describe these taxes or to distinguish them from others.   The best term seems to be "excise" taxes ; this, perhaps, conveys the idea of an arbitrary assessment according to empirical standards.

These taxes may be levied in addition to a regular property tax, or they may be in lieu of all other taxes.   In the latter case no question of double taxation arises, though, of course, equality may be violated, either by an inadequate or an extortionate tax.   In the former case it may be assumed, *primâ facie*, that there is double taxation.   But inequality may not really exist, for these taxes, like taxes on premiums and gross receipts, are often levied in order to reach ability or income which is not affected to a great extent by property taxes.   The same kinds of companies, it will be observed, are liable to these taxes as to the gross receipts and premium taxes.   It may be pointed out that specific amounts which are sometimes thus assessed have the advantage that they escape more surely the danger of being declared taxes on inter-state commerce.

In Minnesota there is an "alternative" tax on the number of tons of ore mined : copper, 50 cents a ton ; iron, 1 cent ; coal, 1 cent, *etc.* These were formerly more common than to-day.

Telegraph companies are commonly taxed according to their wire mileage, as in Alabama, Connecticut, Tennessee and Wisconsin. In Alabama this is in addition to a lump sum ; in Tennessee companies are graded according to their total mileage in four classes, the taxes ranging from $25 to $4,000. In Wisconsin, the tax on the wire mileage is in four classes : first, second, third, and additional wires being taxed respectively, 1 dollar, 50 cents, 25 cents, and 20 cents each. A similar tax is found in Vermont. In Texas the tax is on the number of messages, one cent for each full message, etc. Telephone companies are often similarly taxed ; sometimes the number of instruments or transmitters is the basis, as in Georgia, Tennessee, Texas and Virginia. Express companies and car companies are generally taxed either by a lump sum or by mileage ; in Alabama both are used ; in Tennessee the tax is a lump sum in several classes, according to the mileage. Insurance companies are generally taxed on receipts, as has been already shown, but sometimes by a lump sum, as in Tennessee ; in some cases both kinds of taxes are used, as in Virginia. Another method of taxing insurance companies is upon their policies. Generally there is a certain relation between the value of a company's policies and its taxable ability, but the policies cannot be considered as property. This method of assessment is arbitrary in the same sense as the taxation of telegraph companies according to mileage. Thus, in Massachusetts, life insurance companies are taxed one-fourth percent. on their policies. More in the nature of a property tax, yet distinct from it in the methods of valuation and the rate of taxation, are the taxes on certain assets of insurance companies in Connecticut. The taxation of the deposits of a savings bank at a fixed percentage rate is a property tax in all but its methods of rating ; such taxes are found in Massachusetts and Connecticut. Generally taxes of this kind are levied in addition to the taxes on property. This is the case, for example, in Alabama, Tennessee, Texas and Virginia. In Massachusetts taxes on capital stock are also levied. In Connecticut the taxes assessed on insurance companies, telephone and telegraph companies and savings banks, are in lieu of all other taxes on the property effected thereby. Similarly, in Wisconsin the tax on telegraph .companies is instead of all property tax except that on realty.

Such taxes are generally declared to be on the franchise or the privilege of doing business. In the legal view they have been distinguished from property taxes. The leading cases on this subject have arisen in regard to the taxation of savings bank deposits in Massachusetts and Connecticut. These decisions held that a specific percentage tax on deposits was not a tax on property.[1] More recently the Supreme Court of Connecticut has declared that those doctrines had been pushed to an extreme, and virtually refused to follow them.[2]

Property and Privilege. Corresponding to the taxes on particular occupations through their income are taxes which like them are often termed privilege taxes, but which are assessed by arbitrary methods. They have generally one of two purposes, to operate as a license, or to reach those classes which have income in excess, proportionably to their property. Indicia of the most various kinds are used to determine the amount of the tax, such as the number of rooms in a hotel, the kind and number of animals drawing a vehicle, the seating capacity of a theatre, the number of attachés in a circus, the rental value of a hotel, the number of years of practice of a lawyer, and these may be further rated by the population of the town in which the person resides. In so far as they tax 'the income of occupations, it may generally be said that not

[1] Coite *vs.* Soc. for Savings (1864), 32 Ct., 186, aff'd in Soc. for Savings *vs.* Coite (1867), 6 Wall., 594; Commw. *vs.* Prov. Sav. Inst. (1866), 94 Mass., 312, aff'd in Prov. Inst. Sav. *vs.* Mass. (1867), 6 Wall., 611.

[2] Nichols *vs.* N. H. & N. Co. (1875), 42 Ct., 105.

only double taxation is not produced, but that a more equi-table assessment is made on the taxable capacity of the state. But in so far as they tax the incomes of certain occupations, and allow others needlessly to go free, such taxes cause an in-equality as between occupations, and give rise to double tax-ation. Here, however, the incidence of taxation appears to be more uncertain than usual, and these taxes, as is commonly assumed of licenses, may be largely diffused. Like those priv-. ilege taxes which have the general character of income taxes, they are found chiefly in the southern states.

CHAPTER VI.

JURISDICTION: PROPERTY AND INCOME.

I. WITHIN THE STATE.

Realty. Land in probably every civilized community is subject to taxation, whether owned by residents or non-residents. It would be both impracticable and absurd in the highest degree to demand that a state should be deprived of this source of revenue because the owners were non-residents.

" Land is governed by the law of the place where it is situated."[1] Lands, or immovables, however, are not limited strictly to physical lands, they may include " all other things, though movable in their nature, which by the local law are deemed immovables."[2] Illustrations of this are familiar; among other examples, Story cites mortgages.[3] A striking case is found under the institution of slavery ; " In some states the slaves were regarded as real estate (1 Hurd, Slavery, 239)."[4] It may be stated as a rule, therefore, that " No one can be taxed in respect to his ownership of land unless the land itself is within the jurisdiction of the taxing authority; his personal liability depending on the right to reach and tax the land."[5]

Such is also the law in the United States and the several states.

Tangible Personalty. From an economic point of view

---

[1] Wharton, *Conflict of Laws*, § 273; Westlake, *Priv. Int. Law*, p. 177.

[2] Story, *Conflict of Laws*, ch. xiv, § 551; *cf.* Westlake, *Priv. Int. Law*, § 147.

[3] *Ibid.*, ch. x, § 447.

[4] Springer *vs.* United States (1880), 12 Otto, 586.

[5] Cooley, *Taxation*, p. 393; *cf.* p. 56; Hilliard, *Taxation*, ch. iv, § 65.

there seems to be no practical difference in principle between the rules that should govern the taxation of immovables and movables. That the state should have the sole power to tax its lands is of course of incomparably greater importance.

This, moreover, is not only not repugnant to, but rather in harmony with, the general doctrines of jurisprudence. "A nation within whose territory any personal property is actually situate has an entire dominion over it while therein, in point of sovereignty and jurisdiction, as it has over immovable property situate there."[1] "Whatever the court settles as to the right or title, or whatever disposition it makes of the property by sale, revendication, transfer, or other act, will be held valid in every other country."[2] Wharton in his discussion of this subject denies the application of the maxim that personalty follows the domicile of the owner, in so far as it concerns chattels.[3] He also cites Savigny and many other civilians as maintaining that title to movables is determined by the *lex situs*.[4]

Cooley, on the other hand, as a general principle, approves, rather, of the doctrine *mobilia personam sequuntur* as applied to tangible personalty.[5] Of course, the right of a state to tax personal property actually situated within its confines, if it chooses, is not denied. "So at the option of the state it may impose taxes upon the tangible personal property within the state, irrespective of the residence or allegiance of the owner."[6] "Statutes sometimes provide that tangible personal property shall be assessed wherever in the state it may be, either to the owner himself or to the agent or other person having it in charge; and there is no doubt of their right to do this; whether the owner is resident in the state or not."[7] Such taxes are enforceable against the property itself.[8]

---

[1] Story, *Conflict of Laws*, ch. xiv, § 550.   [2] *Ib.*, ch. xv, § 592.

[3] Wharton, *Conflict of Laws*, § 80, note 2.

[4] Baer, Wächter, Foelix, Fiore, Westlake, Woolsey, *etc.*

[5] Cooley, *Taxation*, p. 371.

[6] *Ibid.*, p. 56.   [7] *Ibid.*, pp. 373-4.   [8] *Ibid.*, p. 21.

In the systems of taxation of the several states, the principle that tangible personal property shall be taxed to non-residents, has been declared by the statutes of most of the states, and upheld as proper in the courts. In many states it is provided that all personal property " in" the state shall be assessed and taxed, *e. g.*, Connecticut, Illinois, Indiana, Kansas, Kentucky, Louisiana, Michigan, New Jersey, New York, North Carolina, Ohio, and in such cases the courts have invariably held that tangible personalty having a permanent location in the state, though owned by non-residents, was in the state within the meaning of the law.[1] Sometimes non-residents are specifically mentioned, as in Maine, California, Georgia and Wisconsin. Again, there is no direct reference to the question of residence, yet the detailed provisions of the tax laws imply it, as in Nebraska, Tennessee and Texas. In Alabama taxation is *in rem*, and non-residents have been judicially declared liable.[2] In Iowa and South Carolina, all personal property is listed by residents, including that in their control. Massachusetts and Rhode Island require the taxation of non-residents on certain specified kinds of property only ; the former requires the taxation of cattle, goods and wares used in merchandising or manufacturing and machinery; the latter, merchandise, stock in trade, lumber and coal, and livery stock permanently located in the state. Pennsylvania taxes chattels locally only (cattle and horses), and non-residents are liable thereon.

The judicial doctrine in the several states is in almost univer-

---

[1] Among the many cases on this point we may cite as leading examples Peo. *vs.* Niles, 35 Cal., 282 ; Shaw *vs.* Hartford, 50 Ct., 530 ; Ins. Co. *vs.* City of Augusta, 50 Ga., 530 ; Dalby *vs.* Peo., 124 Ill., 66 ; Powell *vs.* City, 21 Ind., 335 ; City of Dubuque *vs.* Ry. Co., 47 Ia., 196 ; McCandless *vs.* Carlisle, 32 Kan., 365 ; Meyer *vs.* Pleasant, 41 La. An., 645 ; Leonard *vs.* New Bedford, 82 Mass., 292 ; City of St. Louis *vs.* Ferry Co., 40 Mo., 580 ; State *vs.* McChesney, 6 Vr. (N. J.), 548 ; Peo. *ex rel.* Hoyt *vs.* Comrs., 23 N. Y., 224 ; Bain *vs.* Ry. Co., 105 N. C., 363 ; Carrier *vs.* Gordon, 21 O. S., 605 ; Ry. Co. *vs.* Morrow, 3 Pick (Tenn.), 406 ; Ferris *vs.* Kimble, 75 Tex., 476.

[2] Mayor *vs.* Baldwin (1876), 57 Ala., 61.

sal harmony with this practice, and likewise the doctrines of the United States Supreme Court. In *Coe vs. Errol*, the Court said : " We take it to be a point settled beyond contradiction or question, that a state has jurisdiction of all persons and things within its territory. . . . If the owner of personal property within a state resides in another state which taxes him for that property as a part of his general estate attached to his person, this action of the latter state does not in the least affect the right of the state in which the property is situate to tax it also."[1]   In Massachusetts the doctrine of *mobilia personam sequuntur* prevails in an unusual degree, yet the courts of that state thought that it was " not a violation of any principle of comity to a sister state" to tax property permanently located in the state.[2]   In Missouri it is held that the presumption is that property is located at the residence of the owner, which, if disproven, is " the truth which dispels the fiction."[3]   In North Carolina the court declared that the power and right were beyond " serious question ;"[4] and in an early case in the same state it was held that the fiction that personalty followed the owner had " no application to ' questions of revenue.' "[5]

Choses in Action. The problem here is by no means of equal simplicity with those already discussed, and a satisfactory solution may be admitted to be an impossibility. " No more embarrassing question arises than that which concerns the *situs* of debts. First, where is a debt taxable ?"[6]   Before attempting to answer this question, let us first consider their general economic and legal character.

In the discussion of the propriety of the taxation of property

---

[1] Coe *vs.* Errol (1885), 116 U. S., 517.

[2] Leonard *vs.* City of New Bedford (1860), 82 Mass., 292.

[3] Com. vs. City of Cameron (1885), 19 Mo., App., 573.

[4] Bain *vs.* Ry. Co. (1890), 105 N. C., 363.

[5] Alvany *vs.* Powell (1854), 2 Jo. Eq., 51.

[6] Wharton, *Conflict of Laws*, § 359.

and debts, we concluded that debts in general were not, economically speaking, property *per se*, but merely the claims held by creditors for the transfer of property, actual or potential, held by their debtors. To find the value of the debt, it is necessary to know the means of the debtor, for from his property or income it must be paid. A debt, therefore, in general terms, is an interest in the property of the debtor. As far as it has any *situs*, economically speaking, it is with the property of the debtor, or if he has no property, with his person, for it is to be paid by the transfer of his property, or by his labor.[1] It is evident, however, that this is very indefinite, where the debt is a simple obligation to pay. The debtor might hold property in various places and jurisdictions, or he might reside in various places, and yet he would be equally liable to action for payment of the obligation in any one of them. So in that case its economic situation would be divided, or it would have several situations. Again, a debtor may have no tangible property in his possession, yet ample means to pay the debt; he may be owed values sufficient to pay the debt many times, and his debtors may reside in many different places. Here we may conceive a chain of credits and debts which find their final means of solution in tangible values having an actual physical *situs*. To attempt to fix the ultimate fund or property destined to liquidate such general indebtedness would be chimerical. Such debts for all practical purposes have no *situs* at all; to say they have a *situs* with the creditor is a legal fiction.

With some kinds of indebtedness, however, the economic test of *situs* is practicable. These are claims which have specific tangible values pledged for their redemption. Let us consider first the case of indebtedness, secured by property and without any further obligation or liability whatever on the part of the debtor. It is evident here that, from an economic view, the debt is simply

---

[1] In ancient Rome this is aptly illustrated by the enslavement of the bankrupt debtor.

an interest in the property pledged. The creditor intuitively knows its *situs ;* it is with the pledge, and his interest therein is recognized in many familiar ways by every code of law. What are the principal forms of indebtedness? Mortgage debts, private and corporate, and public stocks. Now all these may be considered to have an economic *situs.* Because with a mortgage there is a note expressing the general obligation of the debtor, is, practically, apart from its legal aspect, a matter of detail. The essential thing is that the debt is secured by definite, tangible values. The mortgage is economically (and it is sometimes declared to be legally) an interest in the land mortgaged. The bonded debts of corporations are the same. If, instead of land, the rolling stock or the revenues of a railroad, or other corporation, be hypothecated, the same principle applies. So it is also with public stocks, whether they be state or municipal. And in the case of public stock it is practicable, and therefore proper, to disregard the fact whether any definite revenues be pledged for their payment or not, simply because there is a tacit contract on the part of the state to raise from its sources of taxation the revenues requisite to meet such obligations, and there can be no ulterior source. Our conclusion, therefore, is this : private mortgages, corporate bonds, public stocks, and any other obligations or claims secured by definite tangible property have their *situs* at the place where such pledge is situated. Purely personal debts, which are not so secured, and which do not form an interest, economically speaking, in any definite tangible property, have no *situs.* For the present we may admit that they might be taxed at the . residence of the owner, so far as the *place* of taxation is concerned.

What is the theory of jurisprudence in respect to debts ? Story under the caption " Situs of Debts," says, " This head respecting contracts in general may be concluded by remarking that contracts respecting personal property and debts are now universally treated as having no *situs* or locality ; and they follow the person of the owner in point of right (*mobilia inhaerent ossibus domini*)."[1] If the contract, however, is prohibited or modified by the law of the state within whose limits the property affected by the contract is situated, then the *lex situs* prevails. "But whatever may be the true rule in cases where the law of the *situs* does not prohibit the contract, as, for instance, a contract for the sale of land, it is very clear that, if prohibited there, it is everywhere invalid to all intents and purposes."[2] The jurisdiction of debts lies, in general, with the *lex domicilii*, but where the contract affects lands in other states, any conditions imposed by the laws of such a state must be observed. So with a mortgage, the law of the state wherein the land is situated may govern the contract; "a mortgage cannot be paid off or extinguished or assigned except in conformity with the *lex situs;* and the *lex situs* must decide whether the contracted act amounts to extinguishment or assignment."[3] "Whether a security given on immovables is governed by the *lex situs* of the immovables is to be determined by that law. If the law says, 'This security is an alienation of the immovables,' then the security is governed by the *lex situs*. . . . The remedy against a mortgagor can be had in any state in which he may be served; though land cannot be proceeded against, except in the *situs*."[4]

There are certain kinds of contracts, however, which are held to be controlled more particularly by the *lex situs*. "It follows as a natural consequence of the rule which we have been considering (that personal property has no locality), that the laws of the owner's domicil should in all cases determine the validity of every transfer, alienation, or disposition made by the owner, whether it be *inter vivos* or *post mortem*. And this is reg-

---

[1] Story, *Conflict of Laws*, ch. viii, § 362; ch. ix, §§ 339, 376, 380; Savigny, *Conflict of Laws*, p. 173.

[2] *Ibid.*, ch. viii, § 373.

[3] Wharton, *Conflict of Laws*, § 292.　　　　[4] *Ibid.*, § 276 a.

ularly true, unless there is some positive or customary law of the country where they are situate, providing for special cases (as is sometimes done), or, from the nature of the particular property, it has necessarily implied locality. Lord Mansfield has mentioned, as among the latter class, contracts respecting the public funds or stocks, the local nature of which requires them to be carried into execution according to the local law. The same rule may properly apply to all other local stock or funds, although of a personal nature, or so made by the local law, such as bank stock, insurance stock, turnpike, canal and bridge shares, and other incorporeal property owing its existence to, or regulated by, peculiar local laws. No positive transfer can be made of such property except in the manner prescribed by the local regulations. But nevertheless contracts to transfer such property would be valid if made according to the *lex domicilii* of the owner, or the *lex loci contractus*, unless such contracts were specially prohibited by the *lex rei sitae;* and the property would be treated as personal, or as real, in the course of administration according to the local law."[1]

Shares of corporations are in some respects similar to obligations. It seems scarcely necessary to argue that they should be considered, economically, to be situated at the place where the corporation's property is situated, or where its business is carried on. It is true that they are technically *choses in action,* but they represent the corporate property, or tangible wealth, which has a definite *situs ;* more strictly they represent an interest therein, which is economically similar to the interest of a partner in the property of the firm. Legally the

---

[1] Story, *Conflict of Laws*, ch. ix, § 383; *cf.* Wharton, *Conflict of Laws*, § 305.

Wharton, in fact, thinks that the doctrine *lex rei sitae* should be applied to movables on political and economic grounds. " But now by far the greater wealth of a nation consists in its public loans and its railway and other securities. By the control of these a foreign sovereign could obtain at least as great political influence among us as by the control of land." *Ibid.*, § 305.

shares of stock are merely evidences of certain rights.[1] Where the maxim *mobilia personam sequuntur* is accepted and generally followed, shares not infrequently form an exception.

In regard to the taxation of obligations, Cooley says, " The mere right of a foreign creditor to receive from his debtor within the state the payment of his demand cannot be sub-jected to taxation within the state." Citing the decision of the United States Supreme Court in the *State Tax on Foreign-Held Bonds Case*,[2] he says, "These are conceded or adjudged principles, and have ceased to be the subject of discussion or argument. Corporations, it is also conceded, may be taxed like natural persons on their property and business. But debts owing to foreign creditors either by corporations or in-dividuals are not subject to taxation. The creditor cannot be taxed, because he is not within the jurisdiction, and the debts cannot be taxed in the debtor's hands through any fiction of the law which is to treat them as being, for this purpose, the property of the debtors."[3] This view of the case is the law, but it is not good political economy.[4] Let the debts, secured by property, be declared an interest in realty, and situated within the state, and the legality of such taxation is indisput-able.[5] This has been the practice in Massachusetts, Oregon

[1] Van Allen *vs.* Assess. (1865), 3 Wall., 273; Peo. *ex rel.* Trowbridge *vs.* Comrs. (1875), 4 Hun., 595.

[2] *Cit. infra.*   [3] Cooley, *Taxation*, p. 21.

[4] Professor Seligman, referring to the decision of the U. S. Court in the *State Tax on Foreign Held Bonds Case*, says: "to the student of political economy the original Pennsylvania decision is far sounder than that rendered by the federal tribunal. . . . From the economic point of view these decisions are indefensible. . . . The bondholders, viewed from the economic standpoint, are no more cred-itors of the corporation than are the stockholders. Both together are co proprietors. . . . It would be far better for the Supreme Court to abandon the whole conten-tion and to reverse its decision on purely economic grounds." Seligman, *Tax-ation of Corp., op. cit.,* pp. 651–6.

[5] When security is given on immovables for a debt which is also personally due, the *lex situs* of the immovables decides whether the debt is to be considered as

and California in respect to mortgages. An examination of the decisions of the United States Supreme Court will also show that " fictions of law " have been used to evade the fiction that personalty follows the owner, where the court found it convenient to do so, although it might with more credit have flatly refused to recognize it.

Shares are usually taxable to the owner at his domicile, under the fiction that they follow his person. According to Judge Cooley, " Shares in a corporation are also the shares of the stockholder wherever he may have his domicile, and if taxed to him as his personal estate are properly taxable by the jurisdiction to which his person is subject, whether the corporation be foreign or domestic. But the state which grants corporate powers, or consents to their being exercised within its limits when the corporate grant is by some other sovereignty, may annex to the grant or consent such terms as it shall deem expedient ; and it may, and sometimes does, provide that the shares of stockholders shall be taxed at the place of corporate business, and the tax be paid by the corporation for all its members. . . . The state may give the shares of stock held by individual stockholders a special or particular *situs* for the purpose of taxation, and may provide special modes for the collection of the tax levied thereon ; and it is often convenient, as well as perfectly just, to take that course."[1] There is no urgent reason why it should be thought desirable that shares should be taxed to the non-resident holders, because they can be reached with equally satisfactory results from the point of view of the economist by taxing the corporation on its property, and to tax both is double taxation. It may be said that this also is true of the non-resident bondholder, *i. e.*, that the corporation shall be taxed on its total property, and

immovable, that is, as an alienation of so much of the value of the immovables on which it is secured, or as a mere debt with collateral security." Westlake, *Private International Law*, § 150.

[1] Cooley, *Taxation*, p. 23.

thereby he shall be indirectly taxed on his interest in the property of the corporation. But this merely bring us back to the old difficulty of taxing property without deducting debts. The shareholder occupies a different position ; his profits will be directly affected, the bondholder will not, unless he is taxed directly, because his interest payment is stipulated in advance, ⁓and, if the tax is paid by the corporation, it will come out of the shareholder.

In all these forms of property having an independent *situs*, it will be noted that the facts are, or may be made, in every case a matter of record ; it is practicable for the tax collector to ascertain from records and accounts under government supervision, the names and interests of those who would be taxable. Those forms of obligations, on the other hand, which are not secured by property, or which are not closely identified with definite property values, are best regarded as having no *situs*. In respect to such property, it is evident that the only place at which it can be taxed is the residence of the owner. In the consideration of debt deduction, no qualification was made, in the assertion that such deductions should be allowed. When more than one state is to be considered, however, the question assumes another aspect. The state cannot allow a deduction of debts from property, where the debt is not itself taxable, *i. e.*, it cannot permit a deduction of unsecured debts due to non-residents.

Under the federal income tax, just held unconstitutional, it is not clear whether the income of non-residents derived from debts owed by persons in the United States, or secured on property therein, is taxable. The statute reads, " He shall include all income from every source, but unless he be a citizen of the United States he shall only pay on that part of the income which is derived from any source in the United States." Bonds and public securities, moreover, are expressly enumerated as " sources " of income. Though the public securities of the United States, however, are expressly exempt, and also

those of the states, by the recent decision of the court, others
still remain besides corporation bonds, *etc.* Arguing from
analogies of foreign laws, such as the English income tax law,[1]
this is entirely within the power of the United States. Leaving
out of consideration the question of citizenship, can this tax
be applied to the income from corporate bonds of non-residents, derived in this country? The decision of the *State Tax
on Foreign-Held Bonds* clearly stands against this, and this decision has been commonly accepted ever since. Nevertheless,
it was actually disregarded in two cases, *viz.*, *Barnes v. Railroad Co.*, and *Railroad Co. v. Collector*.[2] These cases came up
under the former income taxes, which provided for a deduction
of the tax from the interest payments of the bondholders.
The court held that it was an excise on the corporation in
both instances, and refused to meet the question as to whether
it was lawful to tax non-residents on their income from such
bonds. As there is no method of deduction provided under
the present law, the intention of Congress is doubtful. The
income from public stock, however, has been pronounced not
taxable to non-residents[3] in recent decisions respecting the
state tax laws, though very curiously these very obligations
were admitted, *obiter*, to be proper subjects of taxation in the
Foreign-Held Bonds Case. The question of shares in domestic corporations does not come under consideration in this
connection, since the corporations are themselves taxable, and
the dividends therefrom exempt to the shareholder.

In the case of state taxation of federal bonds, it is indeed
questionable, apart from the constitutional objection, whether
they are taxable, according to the principle of economic *situs*.
They are not payable out of the state's treasury. In Maryland the court held them exempt, not because there was an

[1] *Cf.* Dowell, *Income Tax* (1890), pp. 58, 102, 108 (Act 1842, §§ 60, 88, 96.)

[2] Barnes *vs.* Ry. Co., 17 Wall., 294; Ry. Co. *vs.* Collector, 100 U. S., 595.

[3] Murray *vs.* Charleston (1877), 96 U. S., 432; De Vignier *vs.* City of New Orleans (1883), 16 Fed. R., 11.

implied exemption under the constitution, but because they were not a part of the state's resources.[1] In a large sense they are paid in part from the resources of the state, as a portion of the United States. It would not be wrong in principle, therefore, to subject them to state taxation. Residence would, of course, have to be the test, and to this extent it would be inconsistent. But that would be a small matter compared with obtaining a general equality in taxation.

In permitting the taxation of non-resident shareholders on the shares they hold in a national bank Congress has recognized and accepted the doctrine that shares may have an independent *situs*. The Supreme Court has declared this lawful : " the law which creates them may separate them from the person of their owner for the purposes of taxation, and give them a *situs* of their own. . . . A share of bank stock may be in itself intangible, but it represents that which is tangible. It represents money or property invested in the capital stock of the bank. . . . The shareholder is protected in his person by the government at the place where he resides; but his property in this stock is protected at the place where the bank transacts its business."[2]

In the jurisprudence of the several states there is a fairly complete agreement respecting the taxable *situs* of choses in action. Debts are generally declared taxable to residents in express terms ; often they are merely enumerated as species of taxable personalty. In either case, the courts have almost uniformly held that such taxation was applicable to residents only.[3] Debts, as such, are not taxed to non-residents, un-

---

[1] Howell *vs.* State (1845), 3 Gill., 14.

[2] Tappan *vs.* Merchants' Nat. Bk. (1873), 19 Wall., 490.

[3] Peo. *vs.* Park, 23 Cal., 138; Collins *vs.* Miller (1871), 43 Ga., 336; Foresman *vs.* Byrnes (1879), 68 Ind., 472 ; Tax Collector *vs.* Ins. Co. 1890, 42 La. An., 1172; State *vs.* Ross (1852), 3 Zab. (N. J.), 517; Williams *vs.* Bd. Supr. (1879), 78 N. Y., 561; Redmond *vs.* Comrs. (1882), 87 N. C., 122; Meyers *vs.* Seaberger (1887), 45 O. S., 232; Mayor *vs.* Alexander (1882), 10 Lea (Tenn.), 475 ; Ferris *vs.* Kimble (1889), 75 Tex., 476; Comrs. *vs.* Ry. Co. (1876), 27 Gratt., 344; State *vs.* Gaylord (1889), 73 Wis., 316, *etc.*

less they are deemed to have an independent *situs*, which may be acquired in two ways. The first, which is provided for by statute in many states, and approved by the courts, is when they are in the charge of an agent for investment. In that case they follow his domicile. This is found in Illinois, Iowa, Indiana, Kansas, Louisiana, Michigan, Ohio, North Carolina, Tennessee, Texas, *etc*.[1] The second is when they are deposited for safe keeping; in this case the depositary can be looked upon as an agent, as in Louisiana, or the actual paper evidence of the obligation may be considered, as in Kansas.[2] In New York a peculiar statute is found, which renders non-residents taxable on their credits, where they are derived from the sale of lands. They are declared to be personal property where the land is situated.[3] In Pennsylvania, under a former statute, the bonds of non-residents in domestic corporations were made taxable by means of a deduction from the interest payments. This was declared lawful by the state court, though reversed as we have seen in the United States Supreme Court,[4] in the case of *Maltby vs. Reading Ry. Co.* The court said, "It" (the bond) "is founded on and derives its value from a mortgage, but that mortgage is here, and the franchises and properties which the mortgage binds are here within our jurisdiction. The bond signifies his right to receive so much money out of the mortgaged estate, but that estate not only belongs to our jurisdiction, but was in part created by our authority, and the power to raise the mortgage,

---

[1] Goldgart *vs.* Peo. (1883), 106 Ill., 25; Herron *vs.* Keenan (1877), 57 Ind., 472; Hunter *vs.* Bd. Supr. (1871), 33 Ia. 376; Fisher *vs.* Comrs. (1877), 19 Kan., 414; Meyer *vs.* Pleasant (1889), 41 La. An., 645; Curtis *vs.* Richland (1885), 56 Mich., 478; State *vs.* St. L. Co. Ct. (1871), 47 Mo., 594; Redmond *vs.* Comrs. (1882), 87 N. C., 122; Grant *vs.* Jones (1883), 39 O. S., 506, *etc*

[2] Meyer *vs.* Pleasant, *cit. sup.;* Wilcox *vs.* Ellis (1875), 14 Kan, 588; *cf.* State *vs.* St. L. Co. Ct. (1871), 47 Mo., 594.

[3] *N. Y. Laws*, 1851, ch. 371, § 1. *Cf.* Peo. *ex rel.* Jefferson *vs.* Smith, 88 N. Y., 576.

[4] State Tax on Foreign Held Bonds Case, 15 Wall., 300.

like all the franchises of the company, was conferred by state authority."[1]

In regard to the public stock of the states or their local governmental divisions, the accepted doctrine seems to be that they are not taxable to non-residents. In California they were declared taxable in the case of *People vs. Home Insurance Co.* The court said that they were within the jurisdiction of the state : " By seizing and selling the bonds, even if not in themselves property, the thing symbolized or represented by them is seized or sold, and the title of the owners wholly divested and transferred. . . . Whatever the legal fiction as to the *situs* of these stocks, or the thing represented by them, for certain purposes may be, it is plain that there is an actual *situs* within the state, and that the thing constituting the property is within the state and subject to its jurisdiction."[2] In Maryland, laws exist by which the public officers are required to deduct a certain tax from the interest payments, but the courts have denied its application to such portions as are owned by non-residents.[3]

In two states, mortgages are declared an interest in land, and are thereby made taxable to non-resident owners, *viz.*, Massachusetts and California. This avoids the technical legal objections to taxing non-resident bonds.

Shares are a distinct species of choses in action, and the statutes respecting them are more various than respecting obligations. By a federal law the states are permitted to tax the shares of national banks when the bank is located therein, and they have generally been declared taxable in accordance therewith. Shares in domestic corporations are, in a majority of cases, exempt on account of the taxation of the corporations by different methods. But there are frequently some corpora-

[1] Maltby *vs.* Reading Ry. Co. (1866), 52 Pa. St., 140.

[2] Peo. *vs.* Home Ins. Co. (1866), 29 Cal., 533.

[3] App. Tax Ct. *vs.* Paterson (1878), 50 Md., 354; Mayor *vs.* Hussey (1877), 67 Md., 112.

tions which are not taxed directly, in which case the shareholders may be taxed instead. In some states, however, the
non-resident is not lawfully taxable. Thus in Kansas, Massachusetts, New Jersey, North Carolina, Pennsylvania, Texas,
and Wisconsin, *etc.*, such taxation has been disapproved on the
ground that such property is not within the state.[1] Among
those states which tax the shares to the shareholder to some
extent are Alabama, Connecticut, Georgia, Louisiana, Maryland, Missouri, Tennessee, Maine, Vermont, and New Hampshire.[2] It has also been declared legal in Illinois, Iowa, Indiana,
and was formerly so held in Pennsylvania.[3]

In Illinois, in *First National Bank of Mendota vs. Smith*, the
court said that though such property ordinarily followed the
domicile of the owner, positive law could give it an independent *situs*. An important case on this point is *Tax Collector
vs. Insurance Co.* (Louisiana). Shares were distinguished from
debts : " the shares of stock possess inherently only a restricted
negotiability, and transfers of them can be effected *only* by assignment of them, as of other credits, or incorporeal rights.
. . . . To effectuate such transfers, notice to the corporation
is the essence of it, and the only evidence of it is the appropriate entry thereof on the stock books of the corporation, which
are kept for that purpose. . . . . It is a well recognized canon
of construction that credits, incorporeal rights, and things which
are not susceptible of corporeal tradition, may be seized in the

---

[1] Griffith *vs.* Watson (1877), 19 Kan., 23; Oliver *vs.* Washington Mills (1865),
14 Allen (Mass.), 359; State *vs.* Ross (1852), 3 Zab. (N. J.), 517; Ry. *vs.* Comrs.
(1884), 91 N. C., 454; Com. *vs.* Stand. Oil Co. (1882), 101 Pa. St., 119; Rosenberg *vs.* Weekes (1887), 67 Tex., 578; State *vs.* Gaylord (1889), 73 Wis., 316.

[2] Coal Co. *vs.* Comrs., 59 Md., 185; Tax Collector *vs.* Ins. Co. (1890), 42 La.
An., 1172; State *vs.* Rogers (1883), 79 Mo., 283; McLaughlin *vs.* Chadwell
(1872), 7 Heisk (Tenn.), 389.

[3] First Nat. Bk. Mendota *vs.* Smith (1872), 65 Ill., 44; Faxton *vs.* McCosh
(1861), 12 Ia., 527; City Madison *vs.* Whitney (1863), 21 Ind., 261; Whitesell
vs. Northampton Co. (1865), 49 Pa. St., 526.

hands of the custodian thereof if the instrument evidencing the debt or right be *not negotiable.*"[1]

Income. The distinctive income tax is purely personal; it disregards the material sources, and considers only the revenue that persons enjoy.[2] Under such a tax, the pure income tax, non-residents are not taxable on the revenue they acquire from property within the state. This system of taxation, therefore, disregards the economic source of income, and is purely a measurement of the ability of the persons within the jurisdiction of the taxing authority. It is evident that in an extreme case, such as is found in very heavily mortgaged communities, this mode of taxation would be greatly to the financial and economic disadvantage of the state; in wealthy, money-lending communities, on the other hand, it gives a much greater field for taxation. It seems, however, to grossly exaggerate the personal nature of taxes. If it were carried to its logical limits, it would leave untaxed the incomes which non-residents derived from lands within the state. This proves its utter inadequacy as a principle. If, however, the income from such lands be taxed, then, in so far, the personal principle is abandoned, and the economic basis of taxation recognized. But income taxes, so called, very often do not have the pure income character, but also include the income which non-residents derive from property situated in the state, or the receipts of business transacted therein.[3] If, furthermore, the taxation of residents is limited to that proportion of the income which they acquire from property or business within the state, then the tax, though an income tax in name, is, in scope, identical with the taxation of property *in rem.* The United States has adopted this contradictory and inconsistent method in the in-

---

[1] *Cit. supra.*

[2] An income tax is strictly a personal tax. It asks, how much income has this man? It is regardless of any particular source, but includes all sources.—*Report Maryland Tax Com.*, 1888, p. 183.

[3] *Cf.* the English Income Tax; Dowell, *Income Tax*, p. 222 (Act 1853, § 2).

come tax, but in Massachusetts and Virginia residents only
are taxable on their income.

II. WITHOUT THE STATE.

Realty.   Lands lying abroad owned by a resident of the
state cannot be taxed directly as land.   First, the state has no
jurisdiction over lands without its borders, and every attempt
to establish jurisdiction "must from the very nature of the case
be utterly nugatory."[1]   " Real property out of the state cannot
be taxed to the owner within it."[2]   It is stated that in 1834,
" the commissioners on the revision of the laws of Massachusetts recommended for the consideration of the legislature
that personal estate, shall, for the purposes of taxation, be
construed to include the value of *all lands* without this state,
estimated in money."[3]   No state in the United States attempts
to tax lands lying abroad.

Tangible Personalty.   The state should refrain from any attempt to tax movables situated beyond its confines, for the
same reason that controls it in respect to land so situated.[4]

It has already been sufficiently illustrated that the principles of jurisprudence recognize the propriety of this doctrine,
in considering the taxation of such property situated within the
state.   To say that such property follows the person of the
owner is too unreal a fiction to justify taxation—indeed,
this fiction is constantly losing ground.   " The exceptions
would probably be less frequent if the maxim were *lex situs
mobilia regit.*"[5]   Such taxation seems so obviously unjust
that a maxim should not be allowed to control.   It is true,
nevertheless, that not only is such taxation upheld on that
ground, but is even justified.   "Where one is taxed for his

---

[1] Story, *op. cit.*, chap. xiv, ¿ 551 ; *cf.* Westlake, *Priv. Inter. Law*, p. 178.

[2] Cooley, *Taxation*, p. 56.   [3] *Mass. Tax Report*, 1875, p. 104.

[4] The New York Commission of 1871 declared the taxation of movables situated
without the state as contrary to " the principles of justice and equity." p. 44.

[5] Story, *Conflict of Laws*, ¿ 383, note *a* (Bigelow).

personalty at the place of domicile," says Cooley, "it is in general immaterial that some or even the whole of it is at the time out of the state."[1]   "If a person is domiciled within a state, his personal property in contemplation of law has its *situs* there also, and he may taxed in respect of it at the place of his domicile."[2]

The practice in regard to the taxation of tangible movables of residents situated abroad is by no means uniform in the several states, yet, as a general rule, such property is not taxable.   The statutes sometimes express the law directly, as in Connecticut, Maine, South Carolina, Minnesota, Vermont, Rhode Island, Kentucky, Indiana, Michigan and Massachusetts, and here the greatest variety may be found.   Thus in Kentucky, Minnesota, Massachusetts[3] and Maine, tangible personalty abroad is plainly included in the letter of the law. In Indiana and Michigan it is provided that such property as is permanently invested abroad, shall not be included, while in Connecticut, Vermont and New Hampshire, it is not taxable if taxed where actually situated.   In Rhode Island certain kinds of property located abroad are not taxable, *i. e.*, such property as is taxable at home to non-residents.   In South Carolina, the law clearly excludes all property abroad. In other states the real nature of the laws affords the legal presumption that property abroad is not taxable, as in Alabama, Georgia and Ohio.[4]   Sometimes the question turns on the construction as to whether tangible personalty abroad, legally considered, is "in the state;" *e. g.*, New York, North Carolina, Missouri, California, Kansas and Louisiana.   In all these states, the judicial interpretation has been that such property has an actual *situs* abroad and is therefore not tax-

---

[1] Cooley, *Taxation*, p. 371.   [2] *Ibid.*, p. 56.

[3] Bemis *vs.* Boston (1867), 96 Mass., 366.

[4] Varner *vs.* Calhoun (1872), 48 Ala., 178; Collins *vs.* Miller, 43 Ga., 336; Meyers *vs.* Seaberger (1887), 45 O. S., 153.

able.[1] In New Jersey, the statutes seem intended to subject tangible property abroad to taxation, but the courts have construed the language otherwise.[2] In Iowa, Wisconsin and Tennessee, the law does not definitely touch the matter, but the judicial decisions are against such taxation.[3]

Choses in Action. In the discussion of this subject with reference to property within the state, the economic and juristic characteristics of *choses in action* have been sufficiently considered, and the conclusions there arrived at give the rule for taxation here also. Property should not be taxed twice to support the same class of burdens. Therefore, if such obligations as are secured by property in a foreign state are properly taxable by such foreign state, they should not be taxed else-where. A resident should not be taxed on mortgages secured abroad, nor on bonds or shares in foreign corporations, in the state where he resides. Reasons of financial advantage, rather than just principles of taxation, have supported the contrary view. Thus the Massachusetts Tax Commission of 1875 said:: "Neither can we assent to the policy of exempting such property. . . . If Massachusetts were a community with little accumulated wealth, but with natural advantages which needed capital for their development, it might be prudent to join with the demand for such exemption, in the hope that some of our wealthier neighbors would adopt such a .policy and our interests be advanced by the inflow of foreign capital. · But such is not our position . . . very large amounts of capital . . . are used by her citizens . . . in developing the resources and adding to the material wealth of other states."[4] Views of this.

Hoyt *vs.* Com'rs. (1861), 23 N. Y. 224; Alvany *vs.* Powell (1854), 2 Jo. Eq.,. 51; State *vs.* St. L. Co. Ct. (1871), 47 Mo., 594; San Francisco *vs.* Flood (1884),. 64 Cal., 504; Fisher *vs.* Comrs. (1877), 19 Kan., 414; Meyer *vs.* Pleasant (1889), 41 La. An., 645.

[2] State *vs*, Rahway (1853), 4 Zab. (N. J.), 56.

[3] State *vs.* Gaylord, 73 Wis., 316; Bedford *vs.* Mayor (1872), 7 Heisk. (Tenn.),. 409; Rhyno *vs.* Madison Co. (1876), 43 Ia., 632.

[4] *Mass. Tax Report* (1875), pp. 106–7.

character find less acceptance than formerly; the Ohio Tax Commission of 1893 said: "There are many reasons for believing that the taxation of stocks in foreign corporations is impolitic. . . . The question of taxing stocks of foreign corporations is, however, subject to other considerations than those of expediency. If an attempt is made to find an economic basis for this tax, difficulties will be met at once."[1]

The decisions of the United States Supreme Court have quite systematically upheld the taxation of residents on the choses in action, regardless of the character of their economic *situs*. In *Kirtland vs. Hotchkiss*, debts, whether secured by property or not, owing by non-residents to a resident, were held properly taxable, on the general principle that such property had its *situs* at the domicile of the creditor.[2] On the same principle the public stocks of other governments were likewise declared subject to taxation. The court said: " The debt was registered; but that did not prevent it from following the person of the owner. . . . The owner may be compelled to go to the debtor state to get what is owing to him ; but that does not affect his citizenship or domicile."[3] The shares of foreign corporations are held taxable on the same grounds.[4]

In regard to the taxation of the several states, it may be stated as a principle without exception that the general rule is that debts due to residents are taxable, regardless of the residence of the creditor, or the fact that they are secured by property abroad.[5] A special rule is often made in regard to

---

[1] *Report Ohio Tax Com.*, 1893, pp. 65–6.

[2] Kirtland *vs.* Hotchkiss (1879), 100 U. S., 491.

[3] Bonaparte *vs.* Tax Court (1881), 104 U. S., 592.

[4] Sturges *vs.* Carter (1884), 114 U. S., 511.

[5] Mayor *vs.* Baldwin (1876), 57 Ala., 61; San Francisco *vs.* Fry (1883), 63 Cal., 470; Kirtland *vs.* Hotchkiss (1875), 42 Ct., 426; Wright *vs.* Ry. Co. (1880), 64 Ga., 783; Goldgart *vs.* Peo. (1883), 106 Ill., 25; Boyer *vs.* Jones (1860), 14 Ind. 354; Barber *vs.* Farr (1880), 54 Ia., 57; Wilcox *vs.* Ellis (1875), 14 Kan., 588; Com. *vs.* Hayes (1847), 8 B. M. (Ky.), 1; Paving Co. *vs.* City of New Orleans

the credits held by a resident which are in charge of a non-resident agent for investment. This does not include cases where such property is in the agent's hands for collection merely. Indiana, Iowa, Kansas, New York, North Carolina, *etc.*, have made this limitation,[1] and in Connecticut and Ohio it has met the approval of the courts.[2] In Illinois, on the contrary, it has been held immaterial.[3] Sometimes mere deposit abroad has been recognized as removing the credit from the taxing jurisdiction of the state, as in Kansas.[4] In Kentucky, where credits were invested in business abroad, they were held exempt, though this is not the present law in this state.[5] In the case of *People ex rel Jefferson vs. Smith,* the court said, " It cannot be supposed that the legislature intended that our citizens should be subject to taxation here and in other states also upon the same property, or that it would tax in the hands of agents here securities belonging to non-resident owners, while it denied the right of other states to tax the securities of our citizens in the hands of agents there."[6] Under a law in Michigan, now repealed, a very peculiar pro-

---

(1889), 41 La. An., 1015; Howell *vs.* Cassopolis (1877), 35 Mich., 471; Com. *vs.* City of Cameron (1885), 19 Mo. App., 573; State *vs.* Darcey (1888), 51 N. J. L., 140; Peo. *ex rel.* Jefferson *vs.* Smith (1882), 88 N. Y., 576; Redmond *vs.* Comrs. (1882), 87 N. C., 122; Worthington *vs.*, Sebastian (1874), 25 O. St., 1; Com. *vs.* Ry. Co. (1889), 129 Pa. St., 463; Street Ry. Co. *vs.* Morrow (1888), 3 Pickle (Tenn.), 406; Ferris *vs.* Kimble (1889), 75 Tex., 476; State Bk. *vs.* City of Richmond (1884), 79 Va., 113; State *vs.* Gaylord (1889), 73 Wis., 316.

[1] Boyer *vs.* Jones (1860), 14 Ind., 354; Hunter *vs.* Bd. Equal. (1871), 33 Ia., 376; Wilcox *vs.* Ellis (1875), 14 Kan., 588; Peo. *ex rel.* Jefferson *vs.* Smith (1882), 88 N. Y., 576; Redmond *vs.* Comrs. (1882), 87 N. C., 122.

[2] Kirtland *vs.* Hotchkiss (1875), 42 Ct., 426; Worthington *vs.* Sebastian (1874), 25 O. St., 1.

[3] Goldgart *vs.* Peo. (1883), 106 Ill., 25.

[4] Wilcox *vs.* Ellis (1875), 14 Kan., 588.

[5] Com. *vs.* Hayes (1847), 8 B. M. (Ky.), 1. *Cf.* Whitaker *vs.* Brooks (1890), 90 Ky. 68.

[6] Peo. *ex rel.* Jefferson *vs.* Smith (1882), 88 N. Y., 576.

vision existed in respect to the credits of residents secured by mortgage on lands in another state. Mortgages in Michigan, by that law, were declared an interest in the land, and non-resident mortgagees were made taxable thereon. The similar interest of residents was therefore exempted.

Much more diversity exists in the taxation of the shares of foreign corporations. Most states provide that shares of residents shall be taxed without any restriction, except sometimes as regards the shareholders in national banks located in other states (exempt in any case by the federal law), and as we have already seen, they usually exempt the shares of domestic corporations which are taxed directly. In a few states, it is expressly provided that in case the corporations, in which such shares are held, are taxed at their domicile either directly or through the shareholder, then the resident shareholder of such corporation shall not be taxable thereon; *viz.*, Vermont, New Hampshire, and Rhode Island. In California, Connecticut, New Jersey, and New York, they have been declared exempt from taxation by the courts.[1] In California, the federal Circuit Court reversed the decision of the state court;[2] the ground taken being that it was contrary to the Constitution of California. In Louisiana, shares of foreign corporations are apparently not taxable; they are nowhere expressly declared taxable in the laws, and the decision of *Tax Collector vs. Insur. Co.* is consistent therewith.[3] In the leading case in New York, *People ex rel. Trowbridge vs. Commissioners*,[4] the court declared that a share was an interest in the corporation, and that the certificates of stock were not themselves property, and that as the property of the corporation was situated without the state, there was no property " in the state " subject to taxation. The

---

[1] City of San Francisco *vs.* Mackey (1884), 22 Fed. Rep., 602; Lockwood *vs.* Town of Weston (1891), 61 Ct., 211; State *vs.* Ramsey (1892), 54 N. J. L., 546; Peo. *ex rel.* Trowbridge *vs.* Comrs. (1875), 4 Hun., 595.

[2] San Francisco *vs.* Fry (1883), 63 Cal., 470.

[3] Tax Collector *vs.* Ins. Co. (1890). 42 La. An., 1172.   [4] *Cit. sup.*

courts of most states permit the taxation of shares in foreign corporations.[1]

Income. As has been already asserted, the income tax in its pure form is a personal tax, based on the total income of the person taxed as a measure of his ability, without regard to the source whence such income is derived. And though a state, in levying an income tax, may so far depart from its fundamental principles as to tax non-residents on revenues acquired within its territory, it is unusual for them to cut off from taxation revenues of a similar character, of its own residents, which are derived from other states. The Massachusetts commission of 1875 held that taxation found its basis in social necessity, and personal obligation of the persons resident within the state, and that "the income from property outside the state is, on this ground, just as liable to taxation as any other."[2] Such income is taxable under the income taxes of Massachusetts and Virginia, as well as under the federal income tax recently declared to be unconstitutional.[3]

[1] Porter *vs*, Ry. Co. (1875), 76 Ill., 561; Seward *vs*. City of Rising Sun (1881), 79 Ind., 351; Griffith *vs*. Watson (1877), 19 Kan., 23; Dwight *vs*. Boston (1866), 94 Mass., 316; Graham *vs*. Town St. Joseph (1888), 67 Mich., 652; Ogden *vs*. City St. Joseph (1886), 90 Mo., 522; Worth *vs*. Comrs. (1880), 82 N. C., 420; Lee *vs*. Sturges (1889), 46 O. S., 153; McKeen *vs*. Northampton Co. (1865), 49 Pa. St., 519.

[2] *Mass. Tax Report*, 1875, p. 106.

[3] Under the English income tax, only such portion of the income as is received in the United Kingdom is taxable. Colquhoun *vs*. Brooks, Law Rep., 14 App., Cas. 493, cit. in Dowell, *Income Tax*, p. 221.

CHAPTER VII.

CORPORATIONS AND BUSINESS.

I. WITHIN THE STATE.

Property. In the taxation of corporations on their property, justice clearly demands that, whether the corporation
be organized in a given state or not, all its property situated in the state should be assessed to the same extent as the
property of individuals. In the majority of the states, the
general property tax applies to corporations, although special
methods of assessment may be provided. In many states,
however, special corporation taxes have been levied, particularly taxes on capital stock. Foreign or non-resident corporations are often not included in these capital stock taxes, but
are assessed under the general property tax. Where the special corporation taxes do not include foreign corporations, the
general property tax applies in the same manner as to individuals. Such states as do not have any special corporation
taxe, generally provide that corporations shall be taxed on
their personal property at their principal place of business in
the state.

Land is taxed, of course, where it lies; and this is true, indeed, in most cases where the capital stock or franchise tax is
used. In regard to movables, the same rule generally applies
to foreign[1] corporations as to non-resident individuals. Tangible personalty is generally taxable to corporations, if situated in the state.[2] This is specifically provided as to corporations in California, Louisiana, Missouri, New Jersey,

[1] San Francisco *vs.* Mackay, 22 Fed. R., 602.

[2] Ins. Co. *vs.* Assess. (1892), 42 La. An., 760; *cf.* 40 Mo., 580.

Connecticut, South Carolina, Minnesota, Oregon, Arkansas, Washington, West Virginia, Virginia, *etc.* Often they are declared taxable on such property to the same extent as persons, which generally amounts to the same thing; as, for example, in Georgia, Iowa, Texas and Wisconsin. In regard to *choses in action* the same rules apply as to persons. Consequently, non-resident corporations are exempt on their secured credits, except where special conditions exist, as in the case of mortgages in Massachusetts and California. Other special cases exist; for example, in New York, non-residents, private or corporate, are taxable on the capital employed in business in the state. In Louisiana merchants were declared taxable on their property, including credits, employed in business in the state, though such parties might claim a domicile without the state; but this was held illegal.[1] In such states as tax the shareholders in domestic corporations, non-resident corporations, in so far as they hold shares therein, would be likewise taxable; *e. g.*, Vermont and Maryland.

In regard to the rolling stock of railways and car companies, a special problem in respect to *situs* has been encountered. This form of movable property has, from its nature, no permanent location. At first, the tendency was to declare rolling stock non-taxable, if the owner was non-resident;[2] but the better opinion sanctions such taxation to an extent proportional to the amount that such stock is employed in the state.[3] The federal court in *Pullman Car Company vs. Twombly* said, " It is also true . . . . that identically the same cars may not be continously in use in the state of Iowa. But this interchange

[1] Paving Co. *vs.* City of New Orleans (1889), 41 La. An., 1015; Insur. Co. *vs.* Assess. (1892), 44 La. An., 760; Railey *vs.* Assess. (1892), 44 La. An., 765; La. Acts, No. 150, § 1, 9 July, 1890.

[2] Pac. Ry. Co. *vs.* Cass Co. (1873), 53 Mo., 17; Bain *vs.* Ry. Co. (1890), 105 N. C., 363.

[3] State *vs.* St. L. Ry. Co. (1884), 84 Mo., 234; Pullman P. C. Co. *vs.* Twombly (1887), 29 Fed. R., 658.

does not abridge the statement that there is a continuous and constant use in the state of Iowa of the sleeping cars belonging to the complainant." This is the general method of assessing them now practised, and is often required by statute, as, for example, in Georgia, Louisiana, Illinois, Indiana, Arkansas, Missouri, Texas, Tennessee, and Virginia.

The power of the states to tax non-residents or foreign corporations on their property within the jurisdiction of the state is complete.[1]

Capital Stock. Capital stock taxes generally are assessed against resident or domestic corporations, and not against foreign corporations. The latter, in that case, are taxed on their property, instead. These, of course, are not quite the same thing. Neglecting the question of indebtedness, how do they differ? A capital stock tax reaches all the values of the corporation, and includes the franchise, the credits and the tangible property. The property tax, however, in so far as it is applied to foreign corporations, reaches only the realty and tangible personalty situated in the state. The difference is the value of the franchise and credits. If we take indebtedness into account, it appears that in the case of capital stock taxes the value will be diminished, while there is no reduction for that in the assessment of a non-resident's tangible property. Debts, we repeat, will reduce the value of the capital stock; but as the realty is generally assessed independently, this will be of minor importance. It is probably true that the property tax, in the great majority of cases, is less onerous.

The difference between the taxation of foreign corporations on their property and domestic corporations on their stock has been described in *Lee vs. Sturges*, in regard to railroads, as follows. First, as to foreign corporations, the court said : " There is no requirement that it shall list its capital stock, nor, for taxation here, all its property; for that purpose it is

[1] McCullough *vs.* Md. (1823), 4 Wheat., 316; Paul *vs.* Va. (1868), 8 Wall., 168; Pembina M. Co. *vs.* Penna. (1887), 125 U. S., 181.

to return only such as is within the state . . . It may hold millions of credits without the state, and they are not taxed here. Not so, to the same extent at least, with a strictly domestic corporation. Its *situs* is here to all intents and purposes. If it owns credits, shares, for instance, in the stock of foreign corporations . . . it must list the same here as fully as the private citizen is required to do, and of course all visible property is taxed here."[1]

In about half of the states capital stock taxes of a general nature are levied, but these so-called capital stock taxes are often, in reality, rather taxes on property or capital, *i. e.*, a valuation of the total assets with certain deductions. This seems to be the case in Alabama,[2] Ohio,[3] Michigan, Nebraska and West Virginia. In only a few states are foreign corporations included, *e. g.*, New York, Pennsylvania, Kentucky, Minnesota and Tennessee. In Illinois and Indiana it has been held that there was no authority for such taxation.[4] The right to levy such taxes upon foreign corporations has been upheld, nevertheless, by the highest authority. The tax on capital stock, as formerly levied in New York, was assessed against foreign corporations doing business in the state. This was upheld in the state court, as not only legal, but just, in so far as it included foreign corporations.[5] The case was appealed to the United States Supreme Court, which affirmed the judgment of the state court.[6] The statute in question was amended in 1885 to include as taxable stock only such portion as was employed

[1] Lee *vs.* Sturges (1889), 46 O. S., 153.

[2] State *vs.* Ins. Co. (1889), 89 Ala., 335.

[3] Jones *vs.* Davis (1880), 35 O. St., 474.

[4] West. U. T. Co. *vs.* Lieb (1875), 76 Ill., 173; Riley *vs.* W. U. T. Co. (1874), 47 Ind., 511.

[5] "There is no injustice in subjecting to taxation such a corporation enjoying the benefits of our great mart, the advantages of our social order and the protection of our laws."—Peo. *vs.* Horn Silver Mining Co., (1892) 105 N. Y., 76.

[6] Horn Silver Mining Co. *vs.* Wemple (1892), 143 U. S., 305.

in business in the state; the courts have upheld this also.[1]   In
Pennsylvania, the courts have taken the same view, to the extent that foreign corporations were liable on their capital stock
employed in the state.[2]

Receipts and Premiums.   The taxes on receipts and premiums are intended to reach the ability of such corporations as
are inadequately represented, in that respect, by their property.
This is the case with the taxation of insurance companies on
their premiums, and of express, telegraph and telephone companies on their receipts.   Now, it is plain that foreign corporations doing business in a state are especially liable to contribute less than their just proportion if they are taxed merely
on property.   The gross receipts and premium taxes, therefore, include them almost invariably.   In fact, in the case of
insurance companies, foreign corporations exclusively are, in a
few cases, taxed in that manner, *e. g.*, Connecticut, Michigan,
Illinois, Pennsylvania, Kentucky and Ohio.   In a majority of
the states both foreign and domestic companies are taxed.
Such taxes are not, however, levied on all kinds of insurance
companies, and in some cases discrimination is made in the
rates favoring the domestic corporation, as in Massachusetts,
where foreign companies are taxed two per cent. and domestic
companies only one per cent.   This inequality is probably
more apparent than real, because the domestic companies in
Massachusetts are also liable to taxes which are not assessable
to foreign companies.   In Maine, on the other hand, domestic
life insurance companies are taxed and foreign life insurance
companies are not.   Again, in New Jersey domestic life insurance companies are taxed, while similar foreign companies are
exempt, under certain conditions.   This discrimination in New
Jersey is due to certain peculiar laws, which are found in many

[1] Oil Co. *vs.* Wemple (1891), 44 Fed. R., 24.

[2] Com. *vs.* Stand. Oil Co. (1882), 101 Pa. St., 119; Pullman P. C. Co. *vs.* Com.
(1884), 107 Pa. St., 156.

states, which are known as "reciprocity" laws, although retaliatory would be a more accurate term.   These laws provide that if the insurance companies organized within the state are subjected to taxation on account of their business done in another state, then similar insurance companies, organized in the said other state, shall be subjected to the same taxes and fees, on account of any business which they may do in the first-mentioned state.   In New Jersey the domestic life insurance companies, owing to their large business in other states, found that it was more profitable to pay the taxes levied on similar foreign insurance companies in their own state, and thereby purchase an exemption for themselves in all other states having such reciprocity laws.   Reciprocity laws have been generally upheld;[1] in Kansas the court termed them "an appeal for comity; a demand for equality."   In Alabama it was declared unconstitutional as an unlawful delegation of the taxing power, and, also, because it violated the requirement of equality.[2]

Railroads are taxed on their receipts in nine states, telegraph companies in eight states, telephone and car companies in seven states, express companies in ten states, besides miscellaneous corporations, such as oil or pipe line, inter-state bridge, and electric light companies, and others of minor importance, once or more times.   With the exception of foreign railway, canal and steamboat companies in North Carolina, both foreign and domestic companies are equally subject thereto.

Under the United States income tax, recently overturned by the Supreme Court, all corporations doing business within its borders, both foreign and domestic, are liable.

[1] Goldsmith *vs.* Home Ins. Co. (1879), 62 Ga., 379; Home Ins. Co. *vs.* Sargent (1882), 104 Ill., 653; Phœnix Ins. Co. *vs.* Com. (1868), 5 Bush (Ky.), 68; Phœnix Ins. Co. *vs.* Welch (1883), 29 Kan., 672; Peo. *vs.* Ins. Co. (1882), 27 Hun. (N. Y.), 188.

[2] Clark & Murrell *vs.* Port Mobile (1880), 60 Ala., 217.

Specific Taxes. Oftentimes, it is found expedient to make use of specific taxes, in assessing certain corporations. To counterbalance their obvious defects, they have the advantage of being effectively asssssed and, also, escaping many difficulties in regard to inter-state commerce restrictions. They are levied generally on corporations of an inter-state character, such as telegraph, telephone, express, sleeping-car and insurance companies, and are ordinarily imposed alike on domestic and foreign organizations. Conspicuous examples of this method may be found in Alabama, Connecticut, Tennessee, Texas and Wisconsin.

II. WITHOUT THE STATE.

Property. Such states as tax corporations on their property, generally provide that they shall be taxed in the same manner as individuals. This, as a rule, means that real and tangible personal property, situated in the state, and all choses in action, shall be taxed. Realty situated outside of the state cannot be taxed as such[1], and in only a few states, such as Kentucky, Minnesota, and Massachusetts, do the statutes permit the taxation of tangible movables, if permanently situated without the state. Obligations owing by non-residents or secured by property abroad, are usually taxable to corporations as to individuals. In New Jersey, the limitations in the taxation of personal property of residents situated abroad, are held not to apply to corporations.[2] In California, on the other hand, all property situated without the state is exempt to corporations as well as individuals.[3]

Where property, as the rolling stock of railways, is used in several states, it is generally taxed according to the mileage of the railroad in the state; this is the case *e. g.*, in Arkansas and Nebraska and many other states. In Nebraska also, there

[1] Delaware R. R. Tax Case (1873), 18 Wall., 208; Whitaker *vs.* Brooks (1890), 90 Ky., 68.

[2] State *vs.* Metz (1867), 3 Vr. (N. J.), 279.   [3] 63 Cal., 470.

is a special method of taxing sleeping-car and similar companies, on their rolling stock ; the cars are taxed on such portion of their total value as is found by taking the average number employed in the state, together with the average time they are employed therein.

Capital Stock.   Taxes on capital stock are distinguished from taxes on property in different degrees. In some states, they are held to be the same as taxes upon property, as for example, in Pennsylvania, Alabama, Connecticut and Missouri.[1] Where such opinions are held, it would, obviously, be inconsistent with legal principles to tax the total amount, if a portion of the property of the corporation consisted of realty without the state.   In other states, however, the tax on capital stock is held to be a tax on the corporation itself, independent of its property, as in Massachusetts, Delaware and New York.[2] Capital stock taxes may be assessed on the whole amount, or a deduction may be allowed for realty, and the realty, so deductible, may be that portion situated in the state, or the total amount.   If the total amount is deducted, the capital stock tax then takes the form of a property tax.

Considering capital stock alone, in respect to those corporations which possess property or transact business in more than one state, justice requires that only that portion of the capital stock should be assessed which is proportionable to the amount of business done within the state.   Whether the tax be declared a tax on property or on the corporate franchise, the same rule should prevail.   The harmful and unjust consequences of any other position appear, when such a corporation as the Western Union Telegraph Company is considered, a corporation whose business extends to every state in

[1] Com. *vs.* Stand. Oil Co. (1882), 101 Pa. St., 119; State *vs.* Ins. Co. (1889), 89 Ala., 335 ; Nichols *vs.* N. H. & N. Co. (1875), 42 Ct., 105 ; State *vs.* Ry. Co. (1866), 37 Mo., 265.

[2] Com. *vs.* Hamilton Mfg. Co. (1866), 94 Mass., 298; Peo. *vs.* Home Ins. Co. (1883), 92 N. Y., 328; Delaware R. R. Tax Case (1873), 18 Wall., 208.

the Union. It is not sufficient to deduct the real estate, or the tangible property situated abroad, because the most important value is the franchise. Franchises, where they are of great value, as in railroad and telegraph companies, have, as a matter of fact, an actual *situs* as well as real estate; and whether they gain such privileges in a foreign state by an additional act of incorporation in that state or under its general laws, they are just as truly corporations of that state as in the state where they originated, and should be equally subject to taxation.[1] In some states, organizations of that character are specially incorporated, while in others, they operate as foreign corporations. Difficulties in taxation arising in the latter case are commonly settled by taxing them on their property or receipts, and exempting them from the tax on capital stock. This is also true of such organizations as express companies, which are often unincorporated, and have, therefore, no legal franchises, but which possess, nevertheless, a large capital; as their property is of little value, receipts taxes are generally used.

In regard to ordinary business and manufacturing corporations, the greatest disparity exists in respect to the amount of property of a tangible nature situated outside of the state, and, consequently, a great difference as regards the practical justice of assessing all their capital stock. A sugar refining company may have its refineries in several states, and likewise oil companies and brewing and tanning companies. But most corporations have one principal place of business where most of their property is held. They may transact business, however, in other places, as, for example, a manufacturing company situated in one state

---

[1] "The capital stock is taken as the basis of taxation, rather than the road or equipments, for reasons of convenience; but whether the one or the other is selected for the purpose, the limitations of sovereignty alike apply, and the state can tax only what is within its jurisdiction, whether it be the part of the road which is within its limits or the proportion of the stock which represents that part of the road."—*Per* Cooley, J., State Treas. *vs.* Aud. Gen. (1881), 46 Mich., 224.

but selling its goods, to a great extent, in a commercial centre
in another state. This is the most important difficulty in the
question of capital stock taxation. " What business firm or
corporation with ramifications all over the county can tell ex-
actly or even approximately how much of its capital is 'employed' within any one state?"[1] If the firm does a commercial business simply, the sales might be considered to furnish
a fair test. If, however, the goods are manufactured at one
place and sold at another, the method does not apply. Theoretically, a part of the capital can be conceived as engaged
in manufacturing and a part in jobbing. It might be possible,
then, to compare such companies with competing organizations
which undertake such enterprises separately, and tax the given
corporation at its factory, at an amount found by comparison
with the output of similar manufacturing corporations ; and at
its place of sale, tax it on its sales, according to the amounts
levied on similar companies doing the same amount of business. This is a purely empirical method, but, if the original
assumption is correct, it would be approximately just, if it
could be practically carried out. Instead of sales, the average
stock on hand might be used.

The total capital stock is seldom taxed to a corporation
without any deduction for property abroad. This, however,
was the method adopted in New York previous to 1885, and
it was declared lawful by both the state and federal courts,
although the former declared that it was unjust ;[2] " while it is
extremely hard and unjust that the defendant should be required to pay a tax computed upon the basis of its entire capital stock, we are unable so to construe the statute as to relieve
it therefrom." In New Jersey a special franchise tax follows
this principle. No deduction for any property without the
state is allowed, apparently, under the laws of Indiana, Kansas

[1] Seligman, *Taxation of Corp.*, *op. cit.*, p. 649.

[2] Peo. *vs.* Horn Silver Mining Co. (1887), 105 N. Y., 76; aff'd in Horn Silver
Mining Co. *vs.* Wemple (1892), 143 U. S., 305.

and North Carolina. Generally real estate, at least, is deducted; this is provided, for example, in Massachusetts, West
Virginia, New York (local[1]) and New Jersey. Sometimes all
tangible property having a *situs* abroad is deducted, *e. g.*,
Michigan and Nebraska, or, what is practically the same thing,
they may be taxed on the capital stock to the same extent as
individuals are taxable on their property, *e. g.*, Alabama, Illinois and Ohio. In this last case their credits and their other
intangible property values are taxable without regard to the
place where they are derived or employed. All these methods
are evidently imperfect, at least as respects such corporations
whose business is substantially divided in several states. It
should not be understood that all corporations are embraced
under such taxes. Railroads especially are often excepted.

More correct methods have been used in other states. In
Kentucky corporations are taxed on their capital stock and
property employed in the state, which is determined, in part,
by the proportion of gross receipts in the state to the total
gross receipts. In Massachusetts it is specially provided in
regard to telephone companies that they shall be allowed a
deduction from their capital stock of the value of all shares
held in other corporations; this meets the peculiar conditions
of their organization. Taxation of capital stock according
to the proportion of mileage in the state is a common
method in the taxation of railway, telegraph, sleeping car, express and similar companies; it is expressly provided sometimes, as *e. g.*, Connecticut, Massachusetts, Delaware, Maryland and North Carolina. It has generally met the approval
of the courts,[2] as well as of economists. Professor Seligman
says: "Such a standard, while not perfectly exact, is perhaps
as nearly accurate as can be attained."[3] In New York the

[1] Peo. *vs*. Comrs., 104 N. Y., 240.

[2] Atty. Gen. *vs*. Tel. Co. (1891), 141 U. S., 40; Com. *vs*. R. R. Co. (1891),
145 Pa. St. 96.

Seligman, *Taxation of Corp.*, *op. cit.*, p. 649.

statute provides no rule, except that the proportion employed within the state shall be taxed. It has been decided that stock held in a foreign corporation is not an employment of capital without the state.[1] Sales made by a corporation, not at its office in the state, but at its factory in another state, have been declared an illegal basis for taxation.[2] In Pennsylvania, although the statute declared that all capital stock was taxable, the court held that that should not be so construed to be the intention of the legislature.[3]

Receipts and Premiums. It is quite evident that in the taxation of the receipts of companies that do an inter-state business, the assessment should be limited to the receipts which are received for business done within the state, or that proportion of the total receipts which the business done in the state bears to the total business.[4] The methods of business, of course, affect the problem as to what should be the precise method of assessment. Thus, for insurance, and possibly for telegraph and express business, the receipts actually collected in the state would be perhaps a fair measure. With a great inter-state railway or sleeping-car company, the receipts collected in the state might be a smaller part of the total than the proportion of business done therein. The question in this respect seems very intricate. Where the business is carried on over a continuous line, the through business will always be more importantly connected with the terminal portions than with the proportionate parts of the intermediate line. The mileage method, therefore, while a very convenient and proper one, is by no means theoretically correct.[5] In the

---

[1] Peo. *vs.* Wemple (1892), 63 Hun., 444.   [2] *Ibid.*, 133 N. Y., 323.

[3] Com. *vs.* Stand. Oil Co. (1882), 101 Pa. St., 119.

[4] "This phase of double inter-state taxation presents far less difficulties. In regard to gross receipts, the test is a very simple one, *viz.*, the gross receipts from business done within the state."—Seligman, *op. cit.*, p. 656.

[5] Speaking of the taxation of capital stock according to its employment in the state, Prof. Seligman says: "And in the case of telephone companies, the number

insurance business, the *situs* of the risk is a very fair approximation, probably, to the real taxable ability in the several jurisdictions.

In the taxation of premiums, the rule, almost without exception, is to take the portion received from business " within the state," both for foreign and domestic companies. In Georgia and Tennessee it is not expressly declared. As exceptions, in a limited sense, to this rule are Massachusetts, Rhode Island and Louisiana, in which states the assessment is extended to premiums on risks situated abroad, provided they are not elsewhere taxable. The same rule holds in regard to the receipts taxes ; in almost every case it is provided that only that portion received for business within the state shall be taxable. It is not expressly provided in a few cases, *e. g.*, certain local corporations in Georgia, as gas, water and electric light companies, and in certain transportation companies in Virginia. In the assessment various methods may be used ; but in some cases it is specifically provided by statute that the mileage principle shall be applied, *e. g.*, in railroad taxation in Michigan, Vermont, Maine and North Carolina. The late United States income tax law made no provision whatever excluding the income derived from abroad, either for foreign or domestic corporations.

Specific Taxes. Of course, where specific taxes are levied, there may be no possibility of considering the question as to whether the company is taxed on property in another state or not. This is evident where a lump sum is demanded, as, for example, $1000 of express companies in Texas. But where the question of the mileage of a telegraph line or the number of transmitters of a telephone company is introduced, the problem assumes a somewhat different aspect, because then

of instruments used is a better test than the mileage of the telephone wires; for the capital as well as the expenses are in a far more direct proportion to the number of telephones in use than to the amount of wire employed."—Seligman, *Taxation of Corp.*, *op. cit.*, p. 650.

certain positive elements of local value, however variable, are components of the tax valuation. In Alabama, besides a specific sum, express, telegraph and sleeping car companies are taxed one dollar per mile of line within the state. In Connecticut, telegraph companies are taxed twenty-five cents and telephone companies seventy cents on the wire-mileage in the state. In Wisconsin, telegraph companies are required to pay on the wire-mileage in the state, as follows: for the first wire, one dollar, for the second wire, fifty cents, for the third wire twenty-five cents, and for each wire additional, twenty cents. In Texas, telegraph companies are taxed according to the number of messages sent and received in the state; one cent for full-rate messages and one-half cent for half-rate messages. All these rates are, evidently, purely arbitrary in their determination; but whether the taxes are increased or diminished, it is the correct policy to make the basis the property or income, or some portion or function thereof, situated in or derived in the jurisdiction of the state.

CHAPTER VIII.

CONCLUSION.

THE two questions of taxation are, first, what shall be the basis of taxation? *i. e.*, according to what standard of capacity; second, what jurisdiction shall exact the tax? The ideal system is that in which persons are taxed for what they are worth, and at the place where they hold or acquire their wealth. Worth is measured by income or property less debts. The source of wealth is the place where the actual property exists, or where the person performs his labors. If we could satisfy these conditions, neither double taxation nor unequal taxation would exist.

The first difficulty that we meet is that certain kinds of debts cannot be given an economic *situs* with any satisfactory correctness. This makes it necessary to leave out of the scheme of taxation all unsecured debts. It consequently throws out the allowance of a debt deduction for that debt. If the creditor resides in the same taxing jurisdiction, indeed, it might be thought at first that then, in that case, the debt might be deducted; but a little reflection will show that the owner of some tangible property will be liable to lose the deduction which corresponds to the amount thus assessed against the said creditor. Moreover, it would necessitate an inquisition into trade credits which would be impracticable, to say the least, even if the state should refuse to enforce the obligation of such as were not revealed.[1] This difficulty is found in

---

[1] "Auch auf diese aber den gleichen Grundsatz etwa anwenden zu wollen, müsste bei den kaufmännischen und Bankschulden unertraglich werden und

all states and countries. It certainly destroys the possibility of consistent and harmonious application of the principle of debt deduction. The obstacles which we have next to consider are not of a necessary or universal character, but arise from the peculiar political conditions of the United States.

The second difficulty is met in the taxation of corporate bonds. As a general principle of law, secured debts may be taxed at their economic *situs*. They may be declared realty. For such debts, *i. e.*, mortgages, public and corporate bonds, an economic *situs* is possible. These constitute a large proportion of total indebtedness. In the taxation of property by the several states, however, we meet a peculiar legal condition. The most important and extensive corporate bond values in this country are secured on inter-state property. This makes it impossible for the states, separately, to declare them real property, since their jurisdiction is limited to immovables within their own borders.

Third, the bonds issued by the national government, the several states, and other governmental bodies, are to a large extent, within their respective jurisdictions, exempt from taxation.

Here, then, public and corporate bonds, two of the chief forms of indebtedness, are removed, to a large extent, from the power to tax, in those jurisdictions where they have their economic *situs*. Taking the possibilities of debt taxation at the economic *situs*, we have mortgage debts on land in the state, certain non-exempt public bonds, and the bonds of such corporations as are secured by property within the state. This is obviously an unsatisfactory condition. If the debt is not taxable to the creditor, the whole property, without deduction, must be taxed to the legal owner. This would give a very mixed and inconsistent system, and would result in an unequal

wäre auch nur einigermassen wirksam durchzuführen, wenn man den Rechtsschutz verweigerte für den Fall der Steuerhinterziehung."—Schanz, *Finanz-Archiv*, ii, s. 15.

and heavier burden being placed on certain classes of debtors. There would be double taxation in the sense that the debtor, in paying taxes on the property of which he was the legal owner, would be taxed on property which, in an economic view, should be considered the creditor's.

The evident and simple way to solve the difficulty is to refuse to recognize debts as taxable property, and to tax only tangible things. In one sense this avoids all double taxation. If, also, we take into consideration the results of shifting, it may be admitted that to a some extent the result may give a relatively just net income to the creditor and debtor on their respective interests. Certainly it would be much preferable to the present system of partially taxing intangible personalty —the taxation of the honest and evasion by the dishonest— which is objectionable in many ways, but chiefly because of its ineffectiveness. Taxing tangible property only is doubtless much more satisfactory in most respects than a partially successful attempt to reach the ideal. The ideal, however, can be attained to a great extent in such states as are not hampered by the peculiar conditions that confront us in the United States. Is it possible to overcome these difficulties?

We approach this question rather as a matter of speculation than a practical political problem. 'The states are unable to cope with these difficulties. Can the federal government do that which the several states find themselves powerless to effect, because of jurisdictional limitations and constitutional restraints? First let us consider the conditions of the problem.

We have in the United States great corporations, such as railroad, canal, bridge, telegraph, and similar companies, which own vast amounts of property and do an enormous business. Their possessions, which formerly were confined as a rule to a single state, by the extension of their lines, and the consolidation into one of the originally different corporations of the several states, have now frequently been spread over several, sometimes many states. It is especially these corporations which have a large bonded indebtedness. Originally when their possessions were situated in a single state, by appropriate laws, the non-resident as well as the resident bondholder, could have been made taxable by that state. But to-day their loans are secured on the whole corporate property, which extends through different states. Perhaps the state might declare that hereafter no such bonds should be valid, unless certain requirements were complied with. It might demand that the bondholders should be liable to taxation on their bonds; not on the total value—that would be usurpation—but on such part thereof as was in just proportion to the value of the security situated within its borders. It is evident that this, to be even tolerable, would have to be adopted by all the states interested. Or the state might say that no such contracts should be made; that no lien should extend beyond the boundaries of the state. This, however, would involve great embarrassment in procuring loans. Besides, these provisions could act only prospectively, and would leave unaffected the great mass of existing corporate indebtedness for many years to come. The obligation of contract clause in the United States constitution intervenes here to prevent any alteration of existing contracts. The states, we repeat, are practically powerless to deal with the question.

The United States is not. Under the European systems of taxation, and under the income taxes levied both in England and this country, non-residents deriving any income from any source within the state are subjected to taxation thereon. It is well known to what a great extent aliens are investors in American securities; these persons escape taxation within this country. They are not only not taxed at the place where the property is located, but they are not taxed anywhere in the United States. This is a legitimate field of taxation which has long escaped.[1] There would also be many ulterior benefits,

---

[1] "Staatspapiere, Eisenbahnobligationen, Pfandbriefe sammeln sich in den

the need of which has long been recognized. All the questions of the taxation of corporations engaged in inter-state
commerce, of railway employment, and many other matters
that will readily suggest themselves, as well as the matter now
proposed, would be more advantageously controlled. Let the
states, then, exempt from taxation all such corporations as
possess that inter-state character; let the United States levy a
general tax on their capital stockand bonds, and require the
treasurer of the corporation to pay the tax, and give to the
corporation a right to deduct the tax paid on account of such
bonds from the interest paid to the bondholders without regard
to their residence. The proceeds of these taxes could then be
distributed among the several states in which the corporation
operated, according to the extent of their business therein.[1]
The tax so levied could be called a franchise tax on the
corporation,[2] and thus escape the objections presented by the
Foreign Held Bonds Case. Whether this would be declared
illegal as a direct tax, not levied according to the rule of apportionment required by the United States constitution, is not
certain, under the recent decision in the Income Tax cases.

The public bonds which have been declared exempt from

Händen der kapitalkräftigen Staaten, die Hypothekschulden der Landbewohner
sind zu einem grossen Teil in den Händen der Städter oder Angehöriger wohl-
habender Gemeinden. Für die verschuldeten Gemeinwesen ist es von Bedeutung,
die Steuer von dem Zinsertrag, der in ihrem Territorium gewonnen wird, bezw.
von den ihnen wirtschaftlich zugehörigen Personen zu erhalten."—Schanz, *Finanz-
Archiv*, 1892, ii, s. 12.

[1] A similar suggestion to this was made by Prof. Seligman, in respect to the taxation of the receipts of certain inter-state corporations, in order to escape the difficulties attendant on the taxation of receipts of inter-state commerce.—Seligman,
Taxation of Corp. op. cit., p. 464. Dr. Schanz also has suggested a similar method
for such difficulties: " Es ist desshalb am besten, im Gemeindessteuerrecht schlecht-
weg den Kapitalisten am Wohnort zu fassen und bei drückender Lage stark ver-
schuldeter Gemeinden ein zweckmässig ausgebildetes Subventionswesen der
übergeordneten Gemeinschaften eintreten zu lassen (*etc.*)."—Schanz, *Finanz-
Archiv*, 1892, ii, s. 16.

[2] *Cf.* Railroad Co. *vs.* Collector, 100 U. S., 595.

taxation are now beyond the taxing power of either the states or the federal government; in the former case by the prohibition of the constitution of the United States, in the latter by every principle of justice. Henceforth, however, it would be sounder policy to leave such property to the operation of the tax laws of both state and federal governments.[1]

[1] The exemption of such stock is a continual source of fraud and evasion. It should not be exempted. " It was bad financiering, even in the darkest hour of our national struggle, and is wholly inexcusable now " [in case of conversion]. . . . " The rate of interest is far less essential than equality in taxation by which that interest is paid."—A. Walker, *Science of Wealth*, 1866, p. 344.